# POWER OF FAITH

*By Persian Victoria*

## VICTORIA EFTEKHARI

BALBOA.
PRESS
A DIVISION OF HAY HOUSE

Balboa Press books may be ordered through booksellers or by contacting:

Balboa Press
A Division of Hay House
1663 Liberty Drive
Bloomington, IN 47403
www.balboapress.com.au
1-(877) 407-4847

ISBN: 978-1-4525-1094-1 (sc)
ISBN: 978-1-4525-1095-8 (e)

Because of the dynamic nature of the Internet, any web addresses or links contained in this book may have changed since publication and may no longer be valid. The views expressed in this work are solely those of the author and do not necessarily reflect the views of the publisher, and the publisher hereby disclaims any responsibility for them.

The author of this book does not dispense medical advice or prescribe the use of any technique as a form of treatment for physical, emotional, or medical problems without the advice of a physician, either directly or indirectly. The intent of the author is only to offer information of a general nature to help you in your quest for emotional and spiritual well-being. In the event you use any of the information in this book for yourself, which is your constitutional right, the author and the publisher assume no responsibility for your actions.

Any people depicted in stock imagery provided by Thinkstock are models, and such images are being used for illustrative purposes only.
Certain stock imagery © Thinkstock.

Printed in the United States of America

Balboa Press rev. date: 07/16/2013

# FOREWORD

THE TERM PERSIA EVOKES AT once the image of a distant land long ago, and that of a present reality in the heart of Asia, a land joining both geographically and spiritually the Mediterranean world and the universe of Abraham with the Indian subcontinent. Persia is indeed such a reality, a world ancient and contemporary, linked to the heartland of Asia and the cradle of the Mediterranean, a bridge between East and West. Known to the West as Persia until 1935, Iran was occupied by a group of closely related Aryan tribes as early as the 9th century BC. The Persians who eventually attributed the official name of Iran to the country superseded the Medes, who first established an empire, in 550 BC.

The purpose of writing my life story is to be an inspiration to others through their life journey. I am thankful to all the people who have taken part in my journey because they made me into the person that I am today. I apologise in advance if I cause any distress to anyone who is mentioned in my book.

I was born a Muslim and practised the Islamic faith until the age of 40 and even though today I am no longer a practising Muslim, I still read the verses of Koran every night before I go to sleep as it is a part of me and a habit that gives me comfort. I have overcome a lot of emotional hardships in addition to my many physical ailments, sicknesses and 40 operations as well as two major car accidents to get to where I am today. Throughout my life, I have had many near to death but thought nothing of it until the night of my 40th birthday, when, during my nightly prayer, an Angel appeared to me. The Angel, I saw gave me a big tub of golden-like substance and then commenced to pour it all over my body and enlightened me. From that point onwards, I could see and communicate with angels and spirits of the deceased. Until that night, I didn't think or imagine the possibility or existence of such things. I continued on my journey and search for spirituality, which has ultimately led me to become a spiritual healer who believes in God, unconditional love and the Angelic Kingdom and respect all human beliefs. I believe that by using angelic affirmations, it is possible to heal many of my issues, mentally, physically and emotionally. I believe God determines the journey of our life and the only way to go through all the hardship is to accept God's will and destiny, in the other words, Karma. In my opinion, we are as the driver of a car. The roads we travel on are pre-set and we have no choice but to take the journey. Along the way, however, there are cross-roads at which we can make a choice to continue straight on or take a left or right turn.

To be happy, peaceful and healthy needs to be child-like. Look at children, they can fight together and the next minute will cuddle and kiss each others. They fall down and in a few minutes get up and play. I send more prayer and love to people who have hurt me. I believe they need more to join God's light.

When we are born, we are surrounded in God's circle of love and light. As we grow up, we can protect the God's circle of love and light or allow darkness into our life. I survived my life as I state in the God's circle of love and light regardless of what happened in my life. Whilst reading my story, you may come to certain sections that you feel cannot be true or are exaggerated. I cannot believe how I have survived some of the events of my life, by myself as well.

Remembering and writing a true account of my life was extremely emotional and many times brought tears to my eyes and heaviness to my heart. If the reader is a spiritual person, s/he can feel me through their reading of my life story.

## Chapter 1

# My Life in Persia and Overseas

I WAS BORN IN TEHRAN, Iran on 18 August 1951. I was the oldest child in a family of four and I have three younger brothers. I would like to start by writing briefly about my parents' background. My father was born in a wealthy family but he lost tragically his elder brother and sister of an illness and one year later he lost his mother, too, who never recovered after the loss of her children. As a result of that, his father had a massive heart attack and passed away, as well. My father, who was only two years old, went to live with his uncle who was poor and had six children. His uncle had the power of attorney for all the assets left by my father's parents. Unfortunately, the uncle did not take good care of him and thought more of his own children. By the time my father was eighteen, there was only one piece of land left in his name and the rest was spent on his uncle's family. Even though he had a very tragic childhood, he was a caring and compassionate man. He started his own small business and studied in electrical engineering. He continued in building industry and became a very wealthy man. He helped poor and unfortunate people and looked after many families, providing them with home, food, education etc., as there is no social welfare in Iran.

My mother was born into a wealthy family, as well and she was the first child of six. They were four sisters and two brothers. Her father was a very strict man who used physical punishment to discipline her. His idea was to punish her as the oldest child who was responsible for her siblings. One of his punishments would entail tying her to a tree with a rope and then whipping her until she almost fainted. By the age of thirteen, she was forced through a knife to her throat into marriage to a much older man whom she did not love. She also suffered physical and mental abuse during her marriage. The result of this marriage was a girl and my mother was divorced by the age of eighteen and moved back to her parents. She married my father the following year and I was born when she was twenty years old. My half-sister's biological father brought up his daughter from his marriage with my mother. I was unaware of her existence until I was about nine years old, when she came to live with us. We all welcomed her but my mother did not want to even acknowledge her.

I was a very beautiful baby with blond hair and very fair skin like my father, in contrast with my mother, who had olive skin and dark eyes and hair, in a way which people would hardly believe she was my mother. When I was only forty days old, I became very ill with whooping cough, bronchitis that ended up with pneumonia, my mother told. Doctors said that I was going to die and there was nothing that could be done for me. My mother placed me on a blanket on the floor facing Mecca, which is the holy place of Islam, and was praying to God for her daughter's life. After three days of struggling with the illness and shallow breathing, I started to cry and she began to feed me. Because of that, I was susceptible to all kinds of illnesses with a very weak immune system. Consequently, I developed with all sorts of allergic reactions and continuous infections. Despite of all my illnesses, I was a happy and cheerful kid who enjoyed and appreciated just being alive. I was a very friendly and outgoing person with unconditional love and caring toward others and have loved music, dancing and singing.

I've got lost while I was riding my bicycle when I was three years old. In fact, a very rich family, who had no children of their own, had kid napped me and took me to their house. My parents were looking everywhere for me but they could not find me. The family was planning to leave the area with me and they kept me busy playing with toys. One day, the area groceries salesman, who was delivering groceries to their house, recognised me. He called my mother and said "I found Victoria" and he brought her to that house. When my mother saw me playing in there, she was extremely happy to find me but I did not respond to her and she got very upset and the lady told her to leave the house and not to bother them again, pretending I am their daughter. Later on, my father came to the door. I ran to my father's arms and called him "Dad", as soon as I saw him. The family, who had me for those three days, were very upset and offered my parents substantial amount of money to adopt me as their own child but my parents strongly refused.

We had a nice and comfortable house and every Friday, which is the only week-day off in Iran, we had an open welcoming house. All the relatives, friends and neighbours would have come over for lunch and dinner and my parents would enjoy entertaining people.

We had several servants but always one couple of them were living on the premises. The manservant, who was living on the premises, had a daughter the same age as me at the time I was six. Whenever my parents went out at night, he would take his daughter and me to his room while throwing his wife out. He would threaten his daughter and me with a knife and molest both of us. We were so scared, crying quietly and didn't dare to tell anyone as he said he would cut our heads off. This was going on for over four years. When they left, that was the happiest moment of my life and then I dared to tell my parents what he was doing to his daughter and me all these years. My father became too upset and went in search of that man. He would have killed him if other people did not stop him. The man ended up with bone cancer and died after a lot of suffering.

We had a well in our backyard, which was covered by a piece of board I was jumping up and down on its cover board during playing with my brother when I was seven years old. I fell down the well that had a little water as the stream was drying up. I was terrified and injured. It was a miracle that no bones were broken and I suffered no internal injuries. My brother called my Mum and she called a neighbour to help. He brought a long ladder and got me out of the well. As I came outside very traumatised, my mother was very upset with me and I've got a punishment for jumping on the well cover. Later on, my mother took me to a medical centre for a check up. Everything was OK but I had a lot of scratches, aches and pain all over my body.

I was climbing the cherry tree in our backyard to pick up the cherries when I was about nine years old. As I was trying to reach one of the highest branches, the branch broke and I fell down. As my mother had seen that event, she came to me, took the broken branch and wet it and whipped me with that. Then I was put in a dark storage room to be punished for what I did and it didn't matter how much I apologised and I begged her. She was very strict. For example if my brother (who was two years younger than me) or me would use a word like "shut up", we would get punished for it which usually meant putting a hot chilli on our lips and tongues. One day, my mother was so angry with both of us and tried different punishment. She tied me with rope from my shoulders to ankles and hung me upside down in the dried up well which by then was full of different kinds of insects. After a while, just before I nearly passed out, she pulled me out.

My father used to go to work at 6 o'clock in the morning and come back home about 8 o'clock at night, so he was not aware of all these terrible punishments. On one occasion I disobeyed her and went to the backyard to play with my brother. When she found out, she came toward me with a belt. I ran out of the house and went across the road and stayed next to a tree opposite side of our house. She started to throw stones at me but I managed to escape. So finally she gave up and closed the door. I stayed there until 8 pm when my father arrived and asked me what I was doing there. I told him that I ran away because my mother was going to belt me as she always does and I could not take it anymore. So, he held my hand, took me to the house and confronted with my mother. "You are not a man if you don't belt her now for what she has done!" my mother shouted at him, upon seeing us. More so, specifically for running away from the house when in her opinion I should have stayed. My father was so upset and said to her "Isn't all your punishment enough? I can't understand the way you punish your own children. A stepmother would not do what you do". She had a big fight and argument with my father and then decided to leave him because of taking my side. As she started walking out, I ran after her and I begged her to come back. I was sorry to disobey her and said she could hit me if she wanted to and I would never do it again. I was trying my best to obey her wills so I would not get in trouble and the family would not split up. I always tried to control my brother's behaviours as well to stop him of getting into any trouble. One day, however, my brother did something wrong and he got into a big trouble. I tried to cover up for him but it did not work. Therefore my mother brought a knife, put my brother's head in a little garden and pretended to cut his head off. Of course she was using the blunt side of the knife but we didn't realise it. After lots of screaming and begging, she let us both go. We had many of these occasions until I was twelve years old. By then, my father started his new business, which was just across the road from our house. Therefore, he was spending more time with us as we would go and see him in his office any time we wanted. My middle brother was six years old and my youngest brother was one year old. These two younger brothers were never punished in the way my oldest brother and I used to be. The reason was because we were guiding and looking after them and my father was around a lot more by that time.

We had no financial concerns. In fact, we used to go to the private schools and wear the best clothes. We had servants to do all the housework, a personal driver to take us wherever we needed to go and a gardener. We had a very comfortable life in a big and beautiful house. I would say I grew up with lots of money but no love. My mother never hugged or kissed any of us. Her idea of showing a motherly love was to buy us anything we wanted as long as we did what we were told. I felt as though I grew up like a lonely bird in a gold cage. The only way I could survive that childhood period was having my faith in God. I used to pray and cry and ask for help when I was so scared in a dark storage room, and I would feel the warmth all through my body and go to sleep.

I had frequently encountered different kinds of incidents. I suffered from regular bouts of stress and anxiety due to the trauma I experienced as a child and during my adolescence. We used to sleep in the backyard during the warm summer nights. When I was about twelve years old and while I was asleep I felt something stinging on my right thigh. I naturally slapped my hand over my thigh and woke up screaming. My parents came over, put the light on and looked to see what was happening to me. It was a large dead centipede that had all its legs in my thigh. I was bitten by that poisonous insect and had to be taken to hospital for treatment. My leg was quite swollen, I had fever and I was quite sick for a week. About six months after this, as I was riding my bicycle in the neighbourhood, I was badly bitten by a German shepherd that had rabies. I was in pain and bleeding and had to be taken to hospital. Again I was very sick for a couple of weeks.

One day I went to my next-door neighbour who had a heavy iron front gate. The gate caught my left thumb as she closed it and I passed out from pain. Again I had to be taken to hospital. I lost my nail as a result, which now grows crooked. I had a tooth extracted by a dentist after lots of toothache with abscess, which resulted in lots of bleeding. My father had to take me to a medical centre at midnight, as I was unconscious because of huge bleeding. They had to perform emergency surgery that took me over a week to recover.

I had lots of aches and pains all over my body. After the medical check up, the doctor explained that I had extreme calcium deficiency that was resulting in all these aches and pains and because of that my bones were getting very soft. Therefore I needed to take large amounts of calcium supplements for a year to stop further deterioration of the bones.

A kettle with boiling water tipped over on me when I was in the kitchen and my legs were burned from my knees down that took six weeks to recover. I was jumping from a high steel drum, in the other day. As I was trying to jump the height I fell and cut my lower leg so deep that the bone was exposed. I ended up in hospital for another mini surgery.

I fell down and broke my right arm, when I was running. I had to be taken to hospital and my arm was set in plaster. Six months later I broke the same wrist again while I was playing table tennis. My right arm was put in plaster. After that, I was in excruciating pain all the time; even strong painkillers would not take the pain away. After about two weeks, while I was not able to stop screaming, my fingers were turning black. My father took me to emergency centre at midnight. The doctor decided to open the plaster and check my hand. After taking the plaster off, we could see that my whole hand had completely gone black and the doctor said my hand would had to be amputated if we hadn't gone to hospital that night. He reset my hand again and after six weeks my hand healed nicely. From the time he fixed it, I did not have the pain that I had during the previous two weeks. Even after my hand recovered, I realised that I have an excess growth on the side of my wrist, which causes me so many inconvenience up until this day. When I use my hand to write, I become very slow and if I overdo it I always get pain that shoots up my arm all the way to my neck. My father took me back to the doctor and told him about my hand's disability. The doctor said that I had two choices, I could either live with it or he could break the bone again and reset it. I took the first option. I have to give my arm a rest and I have had to learn to live with it.

I have been also continuously suffering from digestive and respiratory problems, which would make problems for me doing everyday activities and travelling. This was a constant source of frustration for my mother.

We went to the seaside in a summer holiday. In fact, the Caspian Sea is the biggest lake of the world and then has no sharks and has very clear water. One day the surf was too big and swimming was not allowed for a period of time. As I was very good swimmer, I went swimming. My brothers and my cousins were at the shallow end but I kept swimming out. Suddenly, I got caught in a whirlpool. I was sucked down and luckily came out of it, but I struggled to get myself back to the beach. My brother realised I was in danger and called the lifesavers that came to me just in time before I passed out and saved me. After that, I've never ever swam in any sea or ocean again.

Education system marks by numbers from 0 to 20, in Iran. I was pressured to get 20 of 20 all the time by my mother. Sometimes, I would get 19 or 19.5 and I would be crying and scared to show it to her. My teachers could not understand why I was so upset while I have the highest mark in the class. I explained that I was scared of my mother. They would give me the 20 and say "Anyway, you get 20 most of the time so I'll give you 20 to get you out of trouble".

One day my uncle had come to visit us with his family. My brother and I wanted to go back to their home, but when everybody sat in the car there was no room for me. My uncle asked me to sit on his lap. My father gave me a dirty look but I did not understand why. When we returned home, my father yelled at me, pulled his belt up and belted me to the stage that I fainted. After a while, he felt guilty and he came and apologised and hugged me and said, "If you obey me, you will not get into trouble".

I was thirteen years old when I got my period for first time, which was another horrific memory. One day I came home from high school and I thought I was bleeding. I kept changing my underwear and again it was full of blood. I had no clue what was going on and was terrified. I thought I am dying. I explained to my mother what was happening to me. She got cranky and shouted at me "shut up and go to your room and stay there". I went to my room and cried and said to myself that my mother doesn't care and I am going to bleed to death. This went on for a couple of hours and then all of a sudden my youngest auntie, who was informed by my mother, came to my room and started to explain to me why I am bleeding. That's how I found out about the monthly menstruation cycle. The way my mother reacted to this made me to think that was a terrible and shameful thing that I had to hide—which I did.

I had a good academic record and I was also good in art (painting, acting, dancing and singing), language and sports (volleyball, high jump and long distance running). I performed on stage at school, at capital theatre as well as on television. I used to also do courses during summer holidays, such as dressmaking and fashion design, hair dressing and make up. At age sixteen I was nominated by the high school for "Teen Princess" in Tehran and this was done through the whole 14 states in Iran. One girl was chosen from each state. This was done during the time of Shah (King) of Iran and Tehran was compatible with big cities in the western world. I became one of the finalists and this did not suit my parents. At the beginning, they allowed me to go because they thought I wouldn't win but as I became one of the finalists, they did not want me to go any further. So, they said "we know you are beautiful and talented but we do not want you to be a Teen Princess in society. You are only our Teen Princess". I was very upset and crying my eyes out and begging them to let me go. The head of the school and the head of the organisation rang them and tried to convince them to allow me to go but they did not agree. I tried to go without their permission. I got dressed up and tried to sneak out of the house. My mother saw me; she slapped me, pulled my hair, dragged me to my room and ripped my clothes off. She also took all my clothes from the cupboard and cut up all my clothes to pieces, locked me inside the room and left. I was devastated and I cried for a long time.

When I was fourteen, I had a friend whom I used to go to school and back with. One day, in our way back to home, I met her brother who was four years older than me and was studying year 11 at high school. At the first look we were very much attracted to each other but nothing happened that time. Later on, one morning when I went to their house, which was in our neighbourhood, he came and opened the door and gave me a letter to say he loved me and he would like to date me. I was very upset how he could even think that way, knowing the culture and the strict upbringing we had. I liked him but I did not dare to even show that to him because I knew that if my parents found out, it would be a big tragedy. I showed the letter to his sister and asked her to speak to him to find out what he had in mind. My friend told him off but she did not let her parents find out about it either. That family, even though they were living in Tehran, had actually migrated from Turkmenistan in Russia. They were from Mongolian race and they were Sunni Muslims. My family were Parsi race and Shia Muslims. His family were very fanatical about their race, religion and culture and they would only allow their children to marry their own kind. Nobody in their family ever married an outsider.

Another friend of mine, who was their cousin, fell in love with a Shia and Parsi boy and she wished to marry him. She informed her parents about her wish and the parents strongly opposed. She told them that if they do not allow her to marry him, she would commit suicide. They told her that dealing with her death is preferable to the shame of such a marriage. Therefore she committed suicide in front of her parents by drinking cyanide. The day before, she told me about her decision. I cried and begged her not to go ahead with it but she was hoping her parents would get frightened and agree to the marriage.

Regardless of all these differences, we gradually got involved. He came to my father and told him that he loved me and wanted to marry me. But I knew my family would not be agreeable with this marriage. However, my father agreed as he was sincere in his feelings towards me and also my father knew that I liked him as well. From the time I was only thirteen lots of different families would come to my parents and ask for my hand in marriage. However, even some of those men were accepted by my parents but because I was not agreeable, they never forced me. When his family found out that we are involved with my family's blessing, they became very upset. One day his father picked his daughter and me up from school to take us home. He dropped off his daughter first and then, instead of taking me home, he took me somewhere into a bush. While he was driving I asked him where we were going and he screamed at me to be quiet. He told me to get out of the car that he wanted to talk to me. I was trembling and crying and so scared. He started to yell at me and tell me how dare I am having relationship with his son. "Don't you know who we are; such a marriage is impossible! You are not one of us and he has to get married to our own kind", he shouted at me. He said he is the head of the Turkmen community in our state and he works with the Royal family and the Parliament and that I am playing with blood! He said during the war he used to bring back a truck loaded with chopped heads of his enemies to his town and would play with those chopped heads. So he finished his sentences by "I hope by now you understand who I am. You have to forget about my son". Then he took me home.

When I arrived home, I ran to my room while crying. I explained what had taken place to my parents who were very worried about my delay, and said "I don't want to see him ever and when he comes, ask him to leave and never come back again, please". He came at his usual time to see me. My parents informed him what had happened regarding his father. He started crying, begged outside my door to accept him as he loves me so much. My parents also kept taking his side but, even at such a young age, I could foresee that there was no future in this relationship and that his parents' disagreement will influence our future.

After that, my father made sure somebody would take me to school and pick me up from school and I never went to their house or accept a lift from any member of their family. About one month later, my fiancé's father came to our door and started talking to my father. He talked in the way he did it to me, threatening my father in the same ways. At the end he said "This marriage will only happen over my dead body." But my father did not take any notice of all his threats and told him to get lost. My father said what is important to him is that his son truly wants to marry me and that is all. He said I was not marrying his family! His father said my fiancé had no money and he would take all his belongings away from him and stop all his financial supports. My father said he would support us. Around two weeks after, about 10 o'clock at night, when he was going back to his home, two men attacked him in the dark and bashed him as a warning for his involvement with me. Someone who knew us and witnessed the attack informed us and my father went to help. They tried everything to stop this marriage.

We got engaged when I was 16 years old. In our neighbourhood, across the road from our house, there was a family with a young son about two years older than me who loved me very much. Our families were very close friends, too. We used to go on picnics, trips and used to visit each other frequently. Even though they were aware of my engagement, the whole family were trying very hard to get me for their son. As I went through the trauma with my fiancé's family, I became more attracted to him as his family adored me and loved me so much. In my mind, I would prefer him and his family to my fiancé and his family. After a while my parents realised this attraction between him and me. My bedroom was facing his bedroom and we used to look at each other and wave. Therefore, when my parents realised what was going on, they decided to change my room and put me at the other end of the house so we could not see each other. They almost stopped the friendship. His parents came to our house and tried to talk to my parents and convince them to allow me to marry their son, as they were aware of all the problems with my fiancé's family. But my parents strongly disagreed regardless of my wishes. In my parents' opinion, as I was already engaged, I was committed to marry my fiancé. After this, we stopped all communications. Until one day his mother walked into the house screaming and crying that her son is dying and she begged my parents to allow me to go and talk to him. They let me go in the company of my mother and talk to him. When I arrived there, I found him in bed very weak as he had not been eating and locking himself in his room. He was very happy to see me and I convinced him if he really loved me, he should continue living his life and leave everything in God's hands that there is nothing we could do about this situation. He agreed to continue living and thinking about me.

I was forced to marry a man who I did not want to marry because of all the obstacles. I talked to my parents and begged them to finish this engagement and allow me to get married to the neighbour's son which would be a much happier relationship as his family loved me too, but my parents said that I had to get married to my fiancé and there is no other option. I was very sad and depressed while everybody else was excited about all the wedding arrangements. I decided to stop eating to die. After three days, I could not move out of bed. Finally my grandmother came to my room with some food, held me, cried and begged me to eat and accept this situation and make peace. I agreed and had some food but I was not happy.

Our wedding function took place at a very nice and expensive venue. We had over 300 guests, lots of entertainments and high quality catering. Everyone was happy and enjoying themselves except me. Except my fiancé's younger sister and brother who sneaked out of their house to come at the end of the wedding, nobody from his family attended our wedding. My husband was over the moon. Before the wedding he was worried because he was aware of my feelings toward this marriage. My father paid for all the wedding expenses plus a two-bedroom unit for us to live in. At the end of the party, we went to our unit. As soon as we arrived, I started to cry and tell him that I only married him because my parents forced me to. He kept quiet and went to bed. I went to the balcony and just looked outside, crying and talking to God. This was how my marriage started. I did not know how to cook, how to clean or do any of the normal housework, since I never had to do it before. My parents continued to support us with all the necessities and on daily basis they supplied us with food and money as he was finishing his university degree in architecture.

My father used to come at lunchtime to our place and in the afternoon I would go to my parents' house for dinner. My husband used to come there as well and then after dinner we would go back to our place. I was pregnant and I was very sick. Morning sickness and vomiting were lasting all day and I could only eat lime, apple and dry toast with tea. That would last throughout my pregnancy. I was about four months pregnant when the first death and tragedy occurred in my family. My oldest brother was rebelling and as he reached teenage years, he was all the time fighting with my parents. He started asking for a motorbike when he was seventeen years old. My parents were not agreeable at all but finally they gave in and bought him a very expensive motorbike. He was riding his motorbike and having fun. One of my aunties, who we were very close to, had a thirteen-year-old son. He was very fond of motorbikes, too. On one occasion, he came to our house and asked my brother to take him for a ride. My brother asked him if he had permission from his parents and he said yes. They went for a ride. A car hit them and my cousin fell of the back of the motorbike and was badly injured as he had a recent hernia operation. My brother was thrown up with his motorbike further up the road, as well. They were both taken to hospital but unfortunately and tragically my cousin died. We were all devastated, as we loved him so much. We grew up together very closely and losing him was as painful as losing my own brother, even worse. In fact, my father said "God, why did you not take my son instead of taking their only son". While I was pregnant and sick, having this tragedy to cope with was very hard.

My cousin's father's family held my brother responsible for their son's death and called my brother a murderer. On the other hand when we went to visit my brother in the hospital the first thing he asked was how our cousin was and that he wanted to see him. We had to lie to him as he was in a very bad state; therefore we said they had to move him to another hospital for a specific operation. Police got involved with the case and straight away they wanted to charge my brother for the accident, which resulted in my cousin's death. My father had to put up bail for my brother while he was recovering in hospital and in the meantime we were going every day with a black dress to my auntie's house and silently crying and thereafter changing our clothes and went to visit my brother and acted as if everything was okay. He would constantly inquire about our cousin and we would lie and say that he was getting better. After about two weeks, when he was on crutches, we took him home. He insisted on talking to my auntie who he loved very much. When my brother asked my auntie how is her son, she answered "He is in heaven". The next minute, my brother lost his mind and went wild and uncontrollable. We had to call the doctor and four men finally managed to restrain him. The doctor gave him a strong tranquiliser to calm him down. From that time his life was not the same. He had to go for three weeks to jail. When my aunt's husband found out that he was in jail, he went to court and my brother was released.

After seven months we moved back to my parents' home as they realised I was not coping on my own. I was very happy to be backing home as I knew they were the ones taking care of me and I needed them to survive. I gave birth to my first son when I was eighteen years old. My labour was very traumatic and took 14 hours. My water broke early and the baby was in danger, so I was hysterical. As I was trying to run away from the hospital, they had to tie me to the bed. Twelve hours after starting the labour, the doctor said to my mother, the one was making all the decisions in our lives, I should have a caesarean section as both mine and baby's lives were in danger. My mother strongly opposed this and said I have to have a natural birth and that I will be fine. She was kneeling and praying. Two hours later, I had a son. Only doctors and nurses were allowed into the labour room, as this is the rule in Iran. My son was very healthy, weighing 3.2 kg. He was circumcised when he was three days old as is the Muslim custom. I breast-fed him as I had lots of milk. I went home with the baby. Thanks God! He was a healthy baby not sick like his mother.

I had to deal with motherhood plus having mastitis and gynaecological infections. Therefore my stiches took much longer to heal than normal. Because of the baby, I did not want to take any oral medication and only used local medication to ease my pain. I fell pregnant again when baby was only four months old. I was terrified. I could hardly cope with one child. Therefore my husband and I decided to terminate the pregnancy. We kept it to ourselves because we knew that if my parents found out they would not allow me to have an abortion. Abortion is illegal except in life threatening situations, in Iran. However, we had to find a doctor to perform the procedure. There was a doctor who was illegally doing it in a room at the back of his surgery for quite a substantial amount of money. We had to sign a release form exempting him from any responsibility regarding this procedure. We went through with this arrangement. I was under local anaesthetic that meant I could see everything and partially feel the pain. I had the abortion then I was taken home. As a result of this abortion, I ended up with an infection, which was close to kill me. Therefore my parents found out and were very angry with both of us. I was still breastfeeding my son with lots of difficulties.

Four months later, I was pregnant again as I could not use any form of contraceptive because of very bad reaction to all kinds of them. I was pregnant with my second child when I was still recovering from the abortion. As a result, during the nine-month pregnancy, I suffered tremendously and on many occasions, the only choice I had was to run around the house, crying and moaning due to the pain. After the first four months, I had a big abscess on my tooth, which needed immediate operation. So it was performed under local anaesthetic as the abscess was closing my air passage and I had to take some antibiotic to help with the infection.

I had an easy labour with my second child, it only took 2 hours for my second son to be born but the doctor left part of the placenta behind and I nearly bled to death. The doctor tried to fix the problem but he could not. The only choice they had was to massage my stomach very hard to get the piece out. My skin was red, raw and sore for weeks after. It took 24 hours before opening my eyes and finding my mother and all my family members on their knees, praying. I was saved, *a miracle of God*. On the fifth day a qualified nurse gave me an injection and damaged the nerve on my right leg that I ended up limping and having pain for a year. The hospital where I delivered my sons was a private royal hospital with the best doctors and nurses. Hospital accepted responsibility for the damage to my leg and I had physiotherapy three times a week for a year until my leg got better.

I was not feeling good at all and was taking antidepressants. Having two children and a termination within two years, I ended up with many gynaecological problems. I constantly suffered with ovarian, bladder and kidney infection and thrush with lots of pain and discomfort. So I was always on antibiotics, painkillers and other gynaecological medication. I believe my husband went back to his family even though he knew they were against this marriage because he could not cope either and needed his parents' support. When my second son was about four months old, my parents decided to get a nice two-bedroom apartment in north of Tehran to give us more freedom and privacy, hoping that our marriage would survive. My parents thought, by being in our own home, his parents might come to accept our marriage and our children. They did not come around at all and only my husband's siblings came once.

My husband felt happier and took more responsibilities for his family as much as he was capable of. My father still continued to support us financially. After living in our new place for about two months, I was finding it hard to cope with, as I had never had to do any housework including cooking. I managed to look after my children, like breastfeeding, changing and playing with them but I did not know how to cook, clean or shop for groceries. I was not even capable of cooking an egg! Therefore, my parents arranged for somebody to come and clean the house and do the grocery shopping. On many occasions, my parents still supplied our meals. My husband would come home, while I was waiting for him all day, hoping to spend some time with him. About eight o'clock at night he wanted to go to sleep and I had to beg him to go for a simple walk, play chess, or watch a movie together but it was all about him being too tired and not considering his young wife and family needs.

One day I started to get lots of pain and haemorrhaging. I ask my husband to take me to a hospital. At the time, he was watching soccer and replied, "Wait until this game finishes". His friend, who was watching the game with him told him off and said that I did not look well at all. He advised my husband to take me to hospital immediately. He replied again that I'll be OK and able to wait. As the bleeding intensified, his friend did not wait any longer, wrapped me in a blanket and took me to the hospital. As soon as I arrived the doctors said that my bladder had prolapsed and I needed immediate surgery but they could not start operation without my husband's permission. His friend rang him and told him if he didn't get to the hospital as soon as possible, I would die. Therefore he came and signed the permission form for the operation to proceed. My children were terrified and screaming for me. Luckily a neighbour came and took care of them and informed my parents. I had to stay in hospital for two weeks; the operation took almost six hours because of my condition. Later on, at the age of 27 and 32 I had to have the same operation again.

My oldest brother and the whole family went through lots of heartache due to the tragic motorbike accident; therefore he was under the care of psychiatrist and psychologist to help him cope with. It also affected all of us. We lost communication with the closest and the dearest members of our family. My brother had lots of problems with my parents, especially with my mother. On one occasion he was so angry with her that he took her lipstick and wrote all over her bedroom walls and mirrors "Death to the fascist mother" and he ran away from the house. My mother never knew the meaning of love. In her belief, buying expensive things was the only way to show love. None of us remember ever being hugged by our mother. The psychologist suggested that it would help him if he had a female companion. In the other word, he suggested my brother to get married. My mother was strongly against this suggestion. While we were looking for a suitable girl for my brother I asked him what sort of a girl he would be interested in. He replied, "Find someone who looks like you and she must have long hair". My father and I found a beautiful, loving and caring girl for him. I believe she is an earthy angel to save him and without her he could not survive. We went to the girl's family and asked for her hand in marriage. The family accepted pleasantly. It was an arranged marriage, which was a custom in our country. We had an engagement party for them and my mother came to the party very unhappy.

At the time of the engagement my brother and his fiancée met each other for the first time. After the engagement they started to get to know one another and they fell in love very strongly and married the following year. During that year, he started his military service but he was not happy and kept escaping and returning home which extended his military service from the compulsory two years to two and a half years.

One day when he was in a military jail, I decided to go and see the head of the military service. I made an appointment regarding my brother's case without my parents' knowledge and went to his office. When I got there, he said to his soldier to shut the door and asked him not to disturb us. I started to tell my brother's story. While I was crying and asking for his assistance, he came on to me and started touching me. I trembled with fear and realised his intentions. I ran away and kicked the door. The soldier, who was standing outside, opened the door and I ran out and I could hear him yelling at the soldier. After that I never went to anyone for help and I did not mention this incident to anybody. My brother got married during his military service. He continued to be well behaved for the rest of the military service despite all the difficulties.

I had financial support during these hard times but not loving support from anyone. My husband was too young, could not even feel the responsibility for his sons and my father was mostly a father to my sons than their real one. My husband finished his university and had to go to military service. I moved back to my parents' house that was a three-storey building and I was living on the ground floor. For me, all this pain and suffering was too much to cope with and not having the emotional support from my husband. I was so depressed and unhappy that I started to see a psychiatrist and ended up taking lots of antidepressants and sleeping tablets to cope. My husband's family, on the other hand, did not help the situation; even worse, they tried on many occasions to get their son back. One of the occasions was when their second son, who was slightly retarded, was getting engaged to a woman from their own background (my in-laws were first cousins and my brother-in-law also married his first cousin). My sister-in-law rang to talk to my husband and asked him to come to his brother's engagement without me and our children as I was never accepted as part of their family and my children were not "pure blood" according to them either. I found out and I asked my husband if he is going without his family and he replied "of course, I am going. He is my brother!" but I could not agree and said "Why can't we come?" He said that his parents were not allowing it. That night I cried a lot, begged and talked to him all night that "this will fulfil your parents' wish to separate us". But he disagreed. In the morning, his two sisters, his mother and his brother came to pick him up. I got ready and went outside and sat in the car and said, "Wherever my husband goes, I go with him" and I left the kids with my parents. My father was the one advising me to do this. They had no choice but to take me; but during the whole journey, which took eight hours, none of them spoke a word to me and the whole time they were speaking in their own language and my husband was silent and angry with me for forcing myself on them. We were there for two nights and I was a total stranger who was completely ignored by everyone. This occasion happened when I just had my second son; therefore I was still not well enough. One day they had to walk about 5 km to go to the bride's house, some by car some walking and no one offered me a lift. So I started walking, following people. I was bleeding and I felt faint. That was when they called my husband and he had to come and pick me up. He was angry with me thought I should not have come. Some of them found out I was their daughter-in-law but never acknowledged me or introduced me to anybody. We came back from this horrible trip and about a year after the wedding took place. In the meantime, they started to call my husband and invite him over and I did the same thing forcing myself on them as my father advised: "Do not let your husband go there by himself". It was very painful to go to their house, knowing I was not welcome. At the end of the day, when I came back home, I was crying my eyes out and getting more and more depressed. I used to say to my father "Please don't tell me to go. I can't take it. No one talks to me; no one pays any attention to my kids. My children and I are not wanted by that family and they make it very clear". It was more painful to see especially as my husband realised all that and he still wanted to go regardless of me going or not going. His older sister, who was extremely rich as they were involved with the Royal family and lived in a castle, did not help our situation at all. She could easily give some financial and emotional assistance to help us, but they did not know the meaning of compassion and helping others, not even their own flesh and blood. They even organised for a girl from their background to marry my husband even though he was still married to me and had two children but luckily he did not accept. When his second brother was getting married, they arranged secretly for him to go, making sure I did not find out about the wedding. When I found out my husband had gone to the wedding without informing me, I felt, within my heart, that our marriage was over. I was very hurt and angry. My father arranged transport to take the children and me to attend the wedding. When I got there I was not welcome to go in to their home. One of my husband's aunties, who were feeling sorry for me, accommodated us in her house. My husband found out and he was very angry to see me there but he could not do anything and he came to his auntie's house, too.

His family did not accept our children or me and I could not convince him that if he wanted this marriage to last, he should keep away from them. After all this happened, we started having problems. We loved each other so much; if we did not have all this interfering from his family, our marriage would have lasted forever. When my parents found out about our problems, they tried very hard to solve it. But I was not able to cope anymore since I was very depressed and unhappy. I told my father I wanted a divorce and that I couldn't continue this relationship any longer. My psychiatrist also told my father that the best solution for me would be a divorce; otherwise I would have a nervous breakdown. My father did not accept his advice and said I have to keep my marriage. I didn't agree; he got very angry, belted me and said he would kill me if I ever mentioned divorce again.

I ran away barefoot from the house and got myself to a very close family friend's house. I went to them and explained my situation. They agreed that there was no point in continuing this marriage with all those struggles. They protected me, called my father and informed him of my whereabouts. He came immediately and in front of our friend hugged me and kissed me and said that he was sorry for losing his temper. I trusted him and went home. When we got home I realised he was even more angry. He locked me in a room and said that I was not allowed to go anywhere without him. My children were screaming and calling for me. He was, however, very good to my children and would never hurt them. I stopped eating and said to father "I will not eat until I die". He gave up after three days. He came to my room with some food and cried seeing me so weak. He begged me to eat and accepted my decision, even though it was personally a great shame on him. My husband did not agree with divorce, since there was not any reason for that, from his point of view. Finally I convinced him going back to his family had caused all these problems between us. He should have stuck to his original promise and put the needs of our family first with the knowledge that his family had never accepted me as their daughter-in-law. Thus, we were divorced in 1974.

When I got divorced, our neighbour's son, who previously wanted to marry me, found out, came along and asked me to marry him. But, at the time, he was engaged to another girl who loved him very much. Considering the situation, I refused. One of my father's cousins, who was in love with me all his life and tried very hard to marry me, came along as well and said to me "You know I have lived with thinking about you all my life, even though I am married and have three children but I have never stopped loving you. Even my wife is aware of it". I strongly said "No. I've never loved you the way you love me and I only like you as my cousin." He continued contacting me until this day and every opportunity he had, he approached me. One of my father's friends, who was a dentist and had asked me to marry him prior to my marriage, came along as well and asked to marry me again. I did not agree, as I had no feelings for him. I don't know why my family or I did not accept any of these suitors.

A son of one of my father's workers, whom my parents helped and supported, used to come to our house and spend time with me and my brother as he was in the same age as us. He was very intelligent even though he came from a poor and illiterate background. I had no idea he was in love with me until after my wedding. He tried to commit suicide and I was informed of this through his father after my wedding. He never would dare to tell me how he felt about me as he could only dream about this happing in real life. He wrote a poetry book all about me; in one of the poems, he was walking up the mountain and found one of the most beautiful flowers in the world. He did not know the name of the flower and asked everyone about its name. No one knew, therefore he called it Victoria. He started to write to me when I was living in England.

My father made himself retired from all his work as a building constructor at the age of 45. He built a complex, which had 17 large two-bedroom units and 14 big shops and a factory underneath. So the rent from these properties would leave his family very well off. My father was very successful in his job. He designed and built cities and commercial buildings and he could continue to become a billionaire but his philosophy was "I worked hard and I have more than enough to have a comfortable life for myself and my family, therefore I retire myself and do not want to continue working for greed." His idea was to have more quality time with his wife and his family. In my country there is no social security system or any other kinds of support for poor people. My father was helping hundreds of these poor families. Any woman, who lost her husband and had no support for her family, could go to my father's personal assistant who would put them on a monthly payment for their needs. But he would not allow anybody to know about his charity work. He believed that if you help someone you should keep it to yourself. One day my father came home with no shoes. I asked him what happened to his shoes. He replied he saw a man with no shoes on so he gave him his shoes and some money. He also never treated any of our servants differently to his own family. They always had their dinner with our family. One day one of the king's high officers was invited to our place for dinner. As everybody sat at the dining table, he questioned why the servants were at the dinner table and refused to have dinner at the same table as the servants. My father told him that they were part of the family and always had dinner with us. He felt insulted and left very angry. My father always taught us the same. We are all equal and we should respect each other, regardless of status, colour, religion or race. He truly believed in and practised unconditional love. My mother, on the other hand, was involved with the queen's orphanage organisation and she had committed herself to it. My father did not agree with her activities but not because of her helping the poor. My mother helped lots of unfortunate people but the difference was that she had conditional love. Because of all these differences, regardless of the strong love they had for each other, they got broke apart and it came to the situation when my father asked my mother to stop all these fancy social engagements. My mother refused and, as a result, their marriage fell apart against my father's wishes as my father was strongly against divorce. So my parents got divorced and about two months later was the time my divorce came through

At this stage my youngest brother, who was eleven years old, and my father were living with me and my children. I had finished diploma in medical science and entered to university to become medical doctor. I had to stop during the unplanned pregnancy as I got very sick that couldn't function. My father agreed that I could go to England with my children to continue my studies and he would join us later on as he could not face people after his and my divorce. My youngest brother was very upset and was crying his eyes out for his mother. My father offered my mother to look after him and that he would take care of all their expenses but my mother refused. Even my brother personally begged her to live with her, she still refused. Therefore, I had to become his "mother". I went to England with him and my two children. My middle brother was already sent to England to continue his studies as he was rebelling and not performing well at school in Iran. He was supposed to meet us at Heathrow airport and we were assuming that he was staying in the educational complex in England. When we arrived in London airport, I looked everywhere but there was no sign of my brother. I got upset as I had three children with me, two big suitcases, in a new country and I had no idea where to go or what to do. I was dressed up nicely and I had expensive jewellery on my hands (emerald, diamonds etc). I also had £7,000 cash and about £14,000 in travellers' cheques as I was hoping to buy a house. Before going to England, my father told me not to wear my expensive jewellery as I could lose my life for it. But I replied I had no problem with wearing my jewellery in Iran, therefore how I could have any problems with it in England.

The airport porter came to me and asked if I needed assistance. I accepted and asked for a taxi. I got into the taxi with the three children. Gave him my brother's address and asked him to take me there. He looked at me strangely, which frightened me. The children by then were very tired and sleepy. He took me to my brother's address but unfortunately my brother was not there. They gave me his new address because he had moved. I went to his new address but he was not there either so I left a message with his roommate. I gave him the taxi driver's phone number and address with his permission as he promised to take me around there the next day. I asked the taxi driver to take me to a hotel. He took me to a top hotel in Birmingham. The children were asleep on my lap and I could not leave the taxi so I asked him if he would go in and see if they had a vacancy. He came back and said that they only have one room but they are not allowing the children and me in the same room. I replied that I cannot be separated from my children and he said that this is the rule of the hotel. He could tell that I was an inexperienced traveller and he already had a plan for me. I started crying and asked, "What am I going to do?" He said he has a big house and that he would call his wife and we could stay there for £100 per night. By this time it was midnight and my taxi bill was £580. Even though I was so scared, I had no other choices. Therefore I accepted his offer. Out of desperation, I went to his house with my children. The first thing his wife said when she saw me was that I have beautiful jewellery and touched my diamond necklace. I was even more scared and I took my necklace off and gave it to her. She said that she could not accept such a gift but I insisted that she should have it for their kindness. I put the necklace around her neck and she thanked me. She showed us the room. I put the children into bed and sat on a chair next to the bed and all night I was awake. Occasionally I drifted off to a light sleep. I did not feel safe there. A couple of times the wife came in and asked me why I did not go to sleep. I replied that I was hoping for my brother to contact me. We got up in the morning, got into the taxi with our luggage and the taxi driver started to drive us around trying to find my brother. By the end of the day the taxi fare was another £480 and no sign of my brother. By this time I felt a bit safer with them and I did some grocery shopping and we went back to his house. We had dinner and we talked and at midnight I went to bed. I fell into heavy sleep, as I had not slept for over 48 hours. As I was very tired I left my handbag, with all my documents and belongings, including all the jewellery and money, on the bedside table. I woke up early in the morning and the first thing I looked for was my handbag, which was gone. I started to scream saying, "Where is my handbag" and the family ran into the room and were acting surprised, pretending they did not know what happened. At the same time my brother rang and he immediately came with his friends. He also informed the police about the incident so police arrived after my brother and they assessed the situation. The detective in charge interviewed me and said that it was obvious the taxi driver did the burglary but the police cannot accuse him without any proof. They were saying to the police that the back door had been opened and someone had broken into the house and stole my handbag. The detective said they would just have to investigate. I went through the biggest shock in my life and I was devastated. We had to call my father and explain the situation. My father just said he was glad that nothing happened to any of us and that it is just money. He cancelled all the travellers' cheques and said he would come as soon as he could. I lost all the cash, jewellery and all the documents. I asked for some assistance from the English police but they told me the only thing I can do is to go to the Iranian Embassy in London; they should be able to assist me. I said to my brother if he was at the airport, none of this would have happened. He said he forgot. I was hoping my brother would have enough money to support us until my father arrived but I found out that he had no money. He was sharing a room with a roommate and not even paid his rent. I asked him what happened to all the money that my father sent to him. He answered he had bad luck in gambling! So, instead of studying, as we were led to believe he was doing, he was lying to us and was gambling, drinking and smoking.

We had to move out of the taxi driver's house as they informed me that they were going to Spain for holidays. I contacted the detective and told him. Again he replied that they needed proof to stop him leaving the country. I was so disappointed and shocked by the police treatment; that started my panic attack. My brother found a room in an attic in the south of Birmingham. We went there to talk to the landlord, an Indian man who lived there with his wife and four children. He asked for £60 a week with no bathroom or hot water. Out of desperation, I accepted. I said if he would give us two weeks time then I would pay him double when my father arrived; I explained what happened to us. He agreed, but I did not feel good about him the way he was looking at me. But I felt safe because my brother was there with me. I started to live in that room, which had a broken double bed and a broken single bed with a big hole in the roof and a heater, which only worked when you inserted money in. My brother borrowed some money from a friend and we did some basic grocery shopping, which consisted mainly of bread, jam, honey, cheese, biscuits, chips and tea. It was wintertime and very cold, the temperature would drop to below 11° C. We had only three thin blankets and did not have much money even to use the heather all the time. At night, I would sleep in the middle of my two boys and my 11-year-old brother on the side. My oldest son had problem with bedwetting so practically every night we would get wet. We could not have a shower so I would just wipe ourselves with a wet towel and change clothes. I had to go to local Laundromat to wash our clothes. Also we had to use public amenities to have a bath. We would go there, the attendant would charge £1 per bathtub, so I would get two bathtubs—one to wash ourselves in and one to rinse. I had to wash the dishes in cold water and my hands reacted to the dishwashing detergent, so I developed dermatitis. My hands had never worked before and that was why I was reacting when I started to use my hands for domestic chores.

We had to go to the Iranian Embassy in London; otherwise we could not stay in the country. Therefore all of us, my brother and his friend went to London and tried to see someone in charge in regards to our stolen documents. I spoke to the personal assistant of the Ambassador and explained my situation. He abruptly said there was nothing he could do for us; the only thing he could do was to put us on a military plane and send us back. I went outside, sat on the steps of the Embassy and started crying desperately, talking to God, asking him to help us. All of a sudden, it came to me that before coming to England my father's cousin said to me that if I ever had any problems in England, to go to the Ambassador of the Iranian Embassy because he was like a brother to him as they grew up together. So I went back to the Embassy and straight to the Ambassador's room. The person in charge yelled at me and told me to get out, that I wasn't allowed to come to this area. I yelled back that I was (and I mentioned my father's cousin name) wife and I wanted to see the Ambassador. The Ambassador heard me and came out of his room. He welcomed me very warmly and took me to his room.

I thanked him while I was crying. I told him that I am his friend's cousin, not his wife but I thought that was the only way I could get his attention. When he heard my story, he was very upset with the whole situation. The first thing he did was to call his personal assistant and told him off that his job is to assist people in desperate situations, not to throw them out! He ordered him to issue us with new passports. I showed them the police report regarding the robbery. Therefore we had our passports reissued within one hour. The Ambassador offered to help us with accommodation but I refused and asked him I would appreciate if I could borrow some money to survive and that I would return the money as soon as my father arrived. He lent me £500 and we left the Embassy. The first thing we did was to go to a nice Persian restaurant near the Embassy to have a nice meal. We went back home, I paid my rent to the land lord and I bought a couple of warm blankets. I also did some shopping so that I could do little bit of experimental cooking (as I never in all my life had to cook for myself). My mother was trying to show me how to cook some Persian dishes so at least I had some idea what the meal should look like! I managed to make some food and to learn how to clean, wash etc. It was a huge learning curve for me! This was the beginning of me serving others.

Our Indian land lord, who was married and had four children, was all the time harassing and offering me all his money and himself if I had an affair with him. I kept rejecting him and telling him if he did not stop it, I would go and tell his wife. A young English university student was living in the next room to us and many times, when I cooked, I offered him some food as well and we became friends. My father sent £4,000 to my brother's account and my brother spent some of the money on a car and gambling and gave me about £2,000. Because of that I started to look for a better place to live in and I found an apartment in a better area. I enrolled my children in a day care. My 11-year-old brother and I started English classes at college. I had to be at a bus stop at 6 am, take my sons to the day care which was to the south of the area, then go by another bus to the centre of the city, then change to another bus and go north to my college. On the way back, while I had my books in one hand and some small shopping in the other hand, I needed to go and pick up my sons by 5 pm (they were only two and three and a half years old). When I picked them up, they were tired and wanted me to carry them. So I had to hold them as well as carry the other bags. Couple of the times, I fell down and hurt myself, but I did never let it go of my children; so they were not hurt, ever.

One day my brother and his friend, who used to always come home late at night, did not come at all. In the morning, police came to the door and gave me a notice, which was about my brother having to attend a court hearing. He and his friend were in jail for stealing a car and taking it for a joy ride. I was terrified. I asked the police what I was supposed to do. He said I could come to the court and pay his fine and bail him out as it was his first offence and he was under eighteen. I went to the court. My brother and his friend were escorted to the court house in hand cuffs and were terrified. He started begging and telling me how sorry he was and that he would never ever do anything like that again. The court ended with me paying £1,000 in fines. When we came back home, the land lord said my brother and his friend could not live there anymore. So, we left that place and went to the new place I'd found. Within a week my father arrived and was really upset with my brother.

We started to look for a house to buy. He wanted to buy a big and comfortable house that was in a good location, close to the college, shopping complex and school. We found a beautiful, eleven bedrooms, three bathrooms Victorian house in Sutton Coldfield. It was a very posh and exclusive area where only rich English people lived and we were the only foreigners there. The house initially was for £8,000 on the market that was not an issue for us. We went to a solicitor and asked him to represent us to buy the house. He contacted and informed us two days later that the owners have changed their mind and put the value up to £11,000. My father said he still wanted to buy that house even at that price. The solicitor was advising us against it as it was not ethical to raise the price but my father insisted to buy the house for the safety and the convenience of the location for his children. The solicitor got back to us again and told us the owner raised that price again to £14,000. We knew that he was increasing the price because he did not want a foreigner to come and live in that area. He assumed by increasing the price we would not buy it. After the second rise he gave up and our solicitor went ahead and we bought the house. It was a beautiful spacious three-storey house with a nice big backyard.

We furnished the house hoping for a new start in a new country. The whole neighbourhood never acknowledged or accepted us. I took the master bedroom on the first floor for myself and my two sons. My father, my two brothers and also my brother's friend took the bedrooms on the second floor. We gave the third floor to the English student who used to live next door to us. We made a deal with him; he would help us with our studies and he did not have to pay any rent or board. He accepted this generous offer with pleasure. I had to study plus look after everyone in the household. I had to cook, clean, deal with everybody's problems and be the peacemaker all the time. My oldest brother arrived with his wife six months later. By then they had a baby girl who was only two months old. They left the baby with my brother's mother-in-law because they wanted to study in England. My sister-in-law was very depressed due to her separation from her baby so my father brought the baby to England after four months. They had very strong love and bond between them; however, they had lots of conflicts and differences due to their young age. I would always take her side, which on many occasions my brother would question of my loyalty to him. I always had this sense of fair justice and I would defend the person who was right regardless of who they are.

My middle brother, at the age of eighteen, had got married to a sixteen years old English girl with the permission of her parents, as they loved each other. He had his friend still living with us even after his marriage. He also kept bringing in different friends and I had to cater for all of them. It was a reversal of roles compared to my life in Iran with servants looking after me; I had become a servant to my family. My middle brother was not loyal to his wife and would continue having different girlfriends on the side, which was causing lots of fights and arguments, but, as she loved him deeply, she accepted his way of life. He studied a little and the rest of the time he enjoyed having good time with his friends and gambling. One day I went to the club with him; the manager said my brother has paid for all the new furniture in the club by the money he lost. He was well presented, handsome, very well dressed and he could sweet-talk any woman who he found attractive. He was practising martial art and he had a black belt in Kung Fu. When he was sixteen and had just arrived in England, he went to a pub with his friend and a couple of English youths started picking on them and they left. The young men (there were fourteen of them) followed them outside and beat them up close to death. My brother and his friend had to taken to hospital by ambulance. They had to stay in hospital for three months. That was the reason why he decided to learn martial arts. I believe this incident affected his personality. My father and I were unhappy with his attitude and kept advising him to study and to change his lifestyle, but he never listened.

My youngest brother was going to private school, my sons were enrolled in private preschool and my older brother and sister-in-law and I were going to college to prepare for university. All the schools were within walking distance to our house. My father would come to the college, stay for a while and then go back home to conduct his business from there. One day I had to call the doctor for home visit because everyone was suffering from very bad influenza. They all had very high fever and were in bed. I decided to put everyone in the living room on the floor next to each other so I did not have to keep running up and down the stairs to look after them. When the doctor came, after examining everybody, he checked me as well and said "Do you know that you are in worse condition than all of them?" I replied "But I am OK. I can look after them." He gave me medication for everybody. This lasted about three days and we had many of these occasions in the cold English weather.

The English student who was living with us was pretty healthy and strong. He was vegetarian and practising Hatha yoga and meditation. I also started to do yoga and meditation and became a vegetarian before I left Iran as I was desperate for an answer to all my problems. I heard that yoga was good for body, mind and spirit but due to all other problems, I only managed to do it occasionally. There was an attraction between us and he was feeling sorry for me. He said to my father "Victoria is not a slave; she is a human being and your daughter". I used to pick up my children in the afternoon, bring them home, play and dance with them, feed them, bath them and put them in bed. Then I would do my housework and prepare dinner for the rest of the family. Then I started to study from about 9 pm until 1 or 2 am. I would be up at 6am because the children would wake up early. I could manage on four hours of sleep as I did my yoga and meditation before going to sleep but I could never do it as well as he did, since I was only a beginner. My mother came to visit us but not in any way helping me to take care of the family. In fact, she criticised me and believed I am interfering in her family's life. They were old enough to take care of themself and I should not be mothering them. She was very angry with my brothers who were calling me their second mother. Therefore, she decided to put my youngest brother to royal boarding school where all the princes and princesses from all around the world were studying. We had to buy all his school belonging from Harrods. My brother and I were not happy about this decision but my father agreed with her suggestion as he thought it was too much for me to look after everyone.

My parents went back to Iran. My father still loved my mother and respected her that was why she could still make decision. My children, my brother and I would go to visit my youngest brother on a weekly basis. I also used to call the boarding school during the week and talk with the principal. He was unhappy and wanted to come home every time I visited him. All the other children would just visit their family during school holidays. Within two months, the principal told me my brother was getting very depressed. On many nights, they realised, he put his family picture on his chest and cried himself to sleep. I made the decision to bring him home without my parents consent. Therefore, I went and took all his belongings and brought him home. He was so happy, cuddling, kissing and thanking me. I was happy to have him home and did not care that I had extra work and responsibility. One day, a friend came with her afghan dog that had scabies (we'd never heard of it). The first time I realised there was a problem after about two days of her visit. My sons started to scratch themselves madly so I took them to the doctor. The doctor said that was a disease transferred from an animal. Apparently, this is very contagious and the whole family had to be treated, the house had to be fumigated and we had to be in isolation. No one could come to our place and we were not allowed to go anywhere. A medical team came to the house and treated the whole family for a week. We were not allowed to wash ourselves because of the treatment. It was a horrendous experience for all of us. They also had to do the same treatment to my friend who had the dog. I never allowed any animal in my house after that.

My mother came for another visit. She would take control over our lives, as usual, and instead of thanking me for looking after her children, she would criticise me and interfere. Especially, she was very upset of taking my youngest brother out of the boarding school. My father decided to take my children back to Iran with my mother to give me more time to study as I had lots of exams; and also to give me a chance to think about my future. I did not agree with this decision and could not imagine being away from my children but my father insisted and I could never disobey his decision. My children were with my father for four months. I was missing them desperately, crying all the time, holding their pictures and going to sleep. My father kept telling me that I was still very young and shouldn't be worry about my children. Apparently, when they were in Iran they tried to convince my ex husband and his family to take care of the children but the answer was a direct "No". As I was very worried and scared of not getting my children back, I tried to suicide and took about 80 different tablets and just slept. My middle brother came home, found me and took me to the hospital. They had to pump my stomach out. They said a lot of the tablets were already dissolved and was in my blood system. They had to keep me in hospital for a week for observation. When my father found out, he decided to come back with my children. I was so happy to have my children back.

The English student, who used to live with us, wanted to marry me. He respected my culture and beliefs but he did not like to have any children, even his own; even though I loved him but not to the extent that I would leave my children for him. He did try to cope with my children but it was not in him; the children could feel it and they hated him. Therefore, we decided to go our separate ways. I hoped that he would find a suitable partner. I've never seen him after that.

There were few men among the lecturers and students who liked me and wanted to date me. I had to explain to them that such a thing was not possible considering the Muslim culture and living with my family. One of the lecturers did some enquiries. He found out that if you are interested in a Muslim girl, you need to see and ask her father first. Therefore he came to the house and asked my father permission to get to know my family. I welcomed him and we talked but I said my children were my first priority and I did not want to get involved with anybody until they were older. One of my tutors, who liked me very much and would not take "No" for an answer, decided to send me a very expensive fur coat as a Christmas present. When my father received the parcel (he used to get all the mails, open and then distribute them to us) he came to me straight away, showed me the coat and accused me of sleeping with him because of sending me such an expensive present! He got his belt and belted me until I fainted and it did not matter how much I explained I had nothing to do with him except he was only a teacher to me. But he did not believe me and would not allow me to go to university anymore; and my poor children were witnesses to these happenings. I decided to starve myself. After three days, I was very pale and weak and my father almost cried and begged me to eat. He was taking care of my children as well. After that he would come to the university in the middle of the day to check up on me.

Every morning, my father and my youngest brother would check my clothes and make up, before I got out of the house, because I was not allowed to wear any make up and I had to wear long dresses. So I had to obey otherwise I would not be allowed to leave the house. When I saw the tutor at the university I did not even look at him. He came to me and asked me if I liked his present. I said that I did not. He asked why. I explained it was a very stupid thing to do, that it got me into a lot of trouble and that my father belted me. He insisted that he loved me and he thought that this present would impress me. He was willing to come and talk to my father. I asked him to please forget about it and just to leave me alone but he still decided to come to our house and to explain to my father. Then my father realised that he was sincere and there was nothing between us. He took the whole family out for a dinner and tried to know me better by getting involved with the whole family. After a while, he gave up because he could see that I was not interested in him.

One night I went to disco with my brothers. A man, who was very wealthy and powerful, came over to my brothers and asked if he could dance with me. My brother replied, "No, she will only dance with me". He started talking to my brother and they got involved in some business. That was how he got his way to our house and our family. He would come in his Royce Rolls with his chauffeur and also bring expensive presents for everyone. He took the whole family to clubs and restaurants. Everywhere we went all the staff would respect and acknowledge him. By this time everybody knew he liked me and he did a lot of research about our culture and religion and was very respectful of it. Therefore, one day, he officially asked my father if he could marry me. My family liked him and did not object but I did. After that whenever he came around, I was avoiding him. But he did not give up and started to follow and even threaten me. I did not realise what sort of a man he truly was. He tried to scare me but as he loved me, he would never hurt me or my family. He finally gave up and we never saw him again.

My middle brother was the only person in my family who drank alcohol like water. He's also smoker and used to go to clubs, pubs and discos. He would always be in some sort of trouble or bring trouble home. Sometimes my brother and my father used to bring girls home. I would be serving them and then they would go to their rooms. It was OK for the males to go with different girls but it was a crime if a female would even talk to another man. As usual, one night my brother came home after midnight with a young man, who was a prince from some island. From the first look, he showed interest toward me and continued his very close relationship with my brother. That was the way he was involved with us. As his family was controlling him, very soon they found out that he was involved with my family because of me. Therefore, they warned him to stop this relationship because there was no way they would allow a marriage to a divorced woman with two children. And if he continued they would disown him from everything. Even though, he did not care and he still wanted to marry me. I would not marry him as I already had experience with marriage where the family did not agree with.

My father decided to go for a trip around the world, which was the dream of his life. I was doing my exams. I had to do most of my studies at night so I would not have more than three to four hours of sleep as the children used to wake up at 6 o'clock. During my last exam I collapsed. I was taken to hospital and was put in the ICU for 17 days. I was in coma for those 17 days and I did not remember any of it. My brothers and my sister-in-law, who used to come to visit me, told me that they would just cry and pray for me but I'd never responded to them. After few days my brother called my mother to tell her that I am in hospital and not doing well. My mother answered that if I am really dying then she would come but when they rang my father, who was very hard to track him down as he was on his trip, he came back immediately. The doctors' observation was that I was overworked and exhausted; that was the reason for my unconsciousness.

I was strictly vegan but, as I had to cook meals for my family, I did not have the time to prepare proper vegan meals for myself. Then I was mostly living on herbs, nuts, salads and a little bit of beans and lentils. As I was also taking a lot of medications, I became very sick which I could not even sit or walk. Therefore my father ended up looking after the children and also me. He had to help me even to go to the bathroom. He made me soups that I could hardly eat. He took me to so many doctors and specialists and the end result, after all the checkups, was that I needed good diet with plenty of meat and if I didn't eat meat I would die. All my bones became soft and I was very skinny and underweight. Even just the thought of meat would make me ill. My father would make a soup with vegetable using meat broth but still even this as it hit my stomach I would vomit. Therefore we decided to introduce the meat very slowly, little bit at a time. I contacted many professors who have written a lot of books on vegan and asked them why this was happening to me and no one had an answer. That was why I decided to have little bit of meat once a month with a vegetarian diet and dairy products until this day.

My father sent me back home to Iran for a short break, when I felt a little bit better. I stayed there for two weeks and during this one of my friends, who wrote a poetry book which was all about me, used to come and visit me every day to show his affection for me. When I returned back to England, he continued to stay in touch by letters. During one of my summer holidays, when I came back to Iran, I went for a dinner with him without my father's permission. My father, however, followed me and found out where I went. The next day I was marched to registry office to get married to him and that was how I became married to my second husband. I was shocked but my new husband was happy about the marriage, as this was what he wanted all his life. He was a police officer who worked thousands of kilometres away from Tehran. He had no home or money to support me. He was a typical male chauvinist who had a lot of complex and resentment toward me. Soon after this marriage I went back to England by myself to continue my study.

My big toes, as a result of ingrown nails, became swollen and infected to the degree that my legs would become inflamed. I had to go to hospital and get them both pulled out and this repeated three times in England as well as in Iran. I had to go to hospital to have a curette as I had fibroids in my uterus. There was a girl in the bed next to me with a black baby. She was crying and telling me that she had nowhere to go. She was only 17 and because her baby was from an African man, her family disowned her and she was devastated. I offered her accommodation and that I would look after her and her baby. So I took her home and she stayed with us for six months until she got governmental support and accommodation.

I was constantly suffering from ovary, uterus and bladder infections and all the time was on antibiotics, painkillers etc. which resulted in a very bad kidney problem. The pain was worse than childbirth. I was taken to hospital and stayed for two weeks. They had to give me morphine injections for the pain. I ended up with weak kidneys for the rest of my life and I had to be careful and make sure of drinking 2 to 3 litres of water a day to keep my kidney functioning properly. I suffered with migraine headaches that were so bad. I would vomit and lose my vision and it lasted 1 or 2 days. I was on antidepressants, painkillers and sleeping tablets.

One day, when I went to have a shower, I accidentally turned only the hot water on. I screamed, almost fainted because it was so hot and burnt my face. My father came and wrapped me in a towel and took me to the hospital and I had second-degree burns on my face. My whole face was blistered and badly burnt. I had to go to the hospital every day for 2 weeks to have the dressing changed and over time I recovered very well.

As a result of all these traumas and as I was a very young woman with too much responsibility, it was very hard for me to cope. I am strongly against suicide but the circumstances and my state of mind at the time made me to commit suicide for the second time. First, by holding electrical cord with a wet hand which resulted in being thrown across the room; as this did not work, I jumped from the second storey to the backyard. I was hurt but amazingly I did not suffer any major injury. Then I decided to take tablets again but my brother found me and took me to hospital. This time it was caught at the early stage but they still had to pump my stomach out. The doctors did not release me this time. They transferred me to psychiatrist hospital, as they were worried in case I try again. I was very dopey and sleepy when they transferred me. When I woke up in the morning and I realised where I was, I've got very upset. I said to the nurse "Why am I here? I don't have a mental problem!" She replied as I committed suicide twice, I was a danger to myself and needed help. I insisted to speak to the doctor. They said I would see the doctor for an assessment. As I was walking in the ward, I saw a beautiful baby girl in a cot. I asked the nurse why the baby was there. The nurse said her mother had manic depression and was under lots of medication. She has not have anywhere to go and no one would even accommodate her, while she needs to be accommodated somewhere with people around to look after her and her baby. She had a sister whom the hospital contacted but she was not interested in helping her. The mother came out of her room and looked strangely at me and asked what I wanted. I replied that I had two children and was concerned about her little girl being in this ward. She said that she had no other choices. I offered her that we have a big house and I could look after her and her baby. She looked at me in the way she did not really believe me. I had my assessment with the doctor and the doctor was convinced that I do not have a mental disorder. After listening to my life story, he realised that I was under lots of pressure. Therefore, I was free to go home. I took the mother and her baby with me, too. My father had no objections as he was always helping people as well. I gave her a bedroom but for the first two months she slept in another bed in my bedroom until she was better and I was able to take care of her baby. She reduced her medication until she was free of all the antidepressants. She was happy to have a home and people who took care of her. After a year, she got herself one bedroom housing commission flat and was capable of looking after herself and her baby.

Even though my father provided us with all the necessities it was also lots of limitations. Everything always had to be with his permission, even though all the money was in my account. There were things I would like to do for me or my children but I could not do if he did not agree. As an example, one day I wanted to take the children to the circus and the tickets were a bit expensive. My father said that we could not go as it was not necessary. As I argued with him, he slapped me so hard that I fell off the stairs. I was hurt and also my children witnessed this and were very upset. I decided to do something to get some financial independence. I thought I could buy an English car, drive it back to Iran and sell it. Doing that, I could double my money, pay his money back and have some money for myself. Therefore I purchased a Princess car from British

Leyland and drove with my two boys and my younger brother back to Iran through the whole of Europe during the summer holidays. When I arrived on Turkey's border, the police warned us as one of the Persian drivers who was driving through the mountains back to Iran, was attacked by a gang and killed. As I was driving towards Iran I saw a group of cars waiting in line. They stopped all the cars going to Iran to join them for the safety. When they stopped me and realised that I am a woman, one of the men said, "We are going fast, we can't wait for a woman as it is getting dark". His reason was that women are slow drivers and the rest of the group were male drivers. Some were single and some had their families with them. One man who arrived after me, responded to the conversation "Sorry, but you should ask this lady to drive slower as I have been trying to catch up with her since the last city and I could not". After this I was accepted. The group of nearly 50 cars started to drive towards Iran. On the way, I realised that the car behind me turned off to the wrong road. I thought that the people behind him saw that and somebody would go after him to bring him back, but no one did. So I turned around, followed him and caught up with him and I sounded the horn and put my high beam on so that he would realise what he has done. Then, we both turned around and we caught up with the group. When we arrived at the Iranian border he came out of his car and wanted to kiss my feet. He told off all the men and said, "This lady is more a man than all of you. She saved mine and my family's life." From the border, I continued on to Tehran. I sold the car and made substantial profit, which gave me some financial freedom. My father was very impressed with my decision. I did it without his permission as at that time he was in Iran.

When we went back to England my father agreed that we could do that again for Christmas holidays, but this time we would keep the cars for ourselves. They were the only Princess cars in Iran. My father also brought one of our servants to England, a girl the same age as me, to help with the running of the household in order to give me more time for my studies and to improve my health by having fewer responsibilities. We bought 10 Princesses, 2 Range Rovers and 1 Jaguar from British Leyland. It made a huge impact on the British Leyland as they were not doing very well at the time. They interviewed me, as they never had anybody who would purchase so many cars at once. This interview went to all British newspapers and all the British colonies. Radio and TV stations and some magazines also interviewed me. On Christmas we drove 4 Princess cars back to Iran. I was driving at the front as in charge of our route and the rest were following me, i.e. my father and my brothers. When we arrived to Belgium, on the border they checked all the cars and arrested my father. We were all shocked! So, we asked why they were arresting my father. One of the officers, who could speak English, showed us a picture of a wanted serial killer that looked exactly like my father. So they needed to do further checking, like fingerprinting, DNA test and etc, to ascertain about my father. They kept us for a day while they were doing their investigation. At the end, they apologised to my father and released him. I used to carry large amounts of cash for our day-to-day expenses. We were in Germany, putting petrol in the cars and my father asked me for some money. I gave him about £4,000 and, as we were driving across the highway, I saw my father picking up a young girl hitchhiker. When we arrived to our next stop, which was a nice hotel in Germany, I asked my father why this girl still was with him. He responded, "Because I want her to". I asked him for the money back, as I could not trust that young girl. My father refused to give me the money as it was his money anyway. We registered ourselves in the hotel and went to our rooms. About one hour later, I heard my father screaming that the girl took all his money and the car keys and ran off. My brother and I ran as fast as we could to the hotel-parking garage. We managed to stop her taking the car but she escaped with the money. My father was embarrassed regarding this situation and he never repeated that mistake again. As we were driving through Europe we had a frightening incident in Yugoslavia. It was snowing and very cold (-11 to -14 °C). As I was driving and checking everybody behind me, I saw my father slide off the road and stuck on a little platform (just big enough for a car!) that was just under the edge of the mountain road. We all stopped and I found my father frozen in shock sitting in the car. I stopped a big semi-trailer and asked the driver for assistance. Luckily, he carried long, strong chains and pulled my father out. This was a miracle of God! We continued on our journey. Before we got out of Yugoslavia, a car hit my father's car from the back while we were parked at a rest stop. There was a big damage to the car and, as my father complained, they were blaming him for the accident. They called the police and when the police arrived, they could not speak English but the police also was putting the blame on my father and they decided to take us to the police station in a little village and charged my father. My father was strongly defending himself and it was obvious that the police and the people who hit us were accomplices. They put my father in jail and we parked our cars in front of the police station and spent the night in the cars, as we were all worried about him. In the morning, they held a small hearing in the local court and the judge ruled that my father had to pay £10,000 or stay in jail. We could not understand even one word of what they were saying in the court as all the proceedings were in Yugoslavian. My father was yelling; he was very upset and angry. I had to calm him down and said "Dad, I know this is all planned but we are in the middle of nowhere, they could even kill us and nobody would know, so let's pay the money and get out of here". So, finally my father calmed and agreed, as he was also worried about us. We paid the money and they released him and we continued on our journey. When we were driving through Turkey we stopped at a café for an evening meal. As we started to have our dinner, a big and horrible man came in and pulled my father's hair and pointed at me and asked who I was. My father replied "She is my wife" and he responded, "I want her". My father said he had to fight for me and if he won he could have me. We were so scared but my father did not have any fear to fight him, as he was a very strong man. They went outside in the snow and the whole village came to watch. They fought while it was snowing and very cold. My father won the battle and the man was very embarrassed of losing the fight in front of the whole village. Everybody was cheering for my father. The owner of the restaurant was praising and thanking my father for beating the big man as he was always causing trouble with tourists who were coming to his café. He was a bully, threatening the whole village. After all these problems, we arrived in Tehran safely. After a week my brothers and I returned back to England and my father stayed in Iran.

After 2 months, my father came back to England with a young lady, one year younger than me, and announced "This is my new wife". My brothers and I were speechless. My oldest brother said, "I will never disrespect her but I will never acknowledge her either". My youngest brother was very upset and he ran out of the room. My middle brother and I were shocked but we tried to understand. The household was never the same after this. We constantly had clashes and arguments between us, as her aim was to get rid of all of us and replace herself in my father's life. The first thing my father said in front of all of us was that he did not want to have any more children. He said that he already had all the children he wanted and that he's already told her that. My father asked me to take her to a doctor to get contraceptive pill. I tried to be nice and friendly to her even though it was upsetting for my brothers and my mother to see this relationship. Regardless of all the kindness I was showing her, she was not a nice person. One night my brother was eavesdropping to their conversation and he overheard her telling my father that his children only wanted him for his money and didn't care about him; but she loves him and would give her life for him. She desperately wanted to replace me as my father said on her arrival that I was the lady of the house and therefore in charge of everything. She would do anything to achieve that. Even though I was aware of her plan, I continued to be nice to her. On the outside she would be nice to me but deep down she resented us all. She bought a big baby doll and used to carry it around while bring tears to her eyes, as she so desperately wanted a baby. My father used to respond, "Look dear, if you want a baby you can marry a younger man and I will buy you a house and give you money". But she would respond, "No, I love you and I want to have a baby by you, not any other man".

All her talks affected my father and he was gradually changing to a different person. For example, he would get up in the morning and asking for impossible things to be done right at the moment; if it were not done he would punish us by withholding money or car. My father was a loving, caring and giving person as long as we obeyed him and God help us if we did not! On one occasion my oldest brother had an argument with him and they ended up fighting physically that if I did not throw myself between them, he would have killed my brother. We had lots of these incidents between my two elder brothers and my father because they were not willing to accept all his rules. My oldest brother decided to leave the house and he took his wife and daughter and went to another city to live. They had a lot of hardships for a while as both were university students. After a while I convinced my father to buy a house and help them financially. I had to keep the peace all the time and talk to my brothers and begging them not to argue and disobey. The only way to keep the peace in the household was to obey my father. Later on, my father started to pick on me and argue with me. That was the time and reason we left the house. When we were all gone out of the house, my father's second wife managed to have two boys by my father within a year and that ended their romantic relationship. My father did not have any bitter feelings against the two innocent boys but he was upset because she managed to manipulate him and to do what she wanted. He never trusted her and never gave her any power over his finances.

During another summer holiday I received 2 other Princess cars and a Range Rover. We decided to go back home in these cars. My eldest brother and his wife were in one car, my middle brother and his girlfriend were in the second and I drove the Range Rover. I was supposed to go with my two sons and the young servant. Few nights prior to our trip, I had a dream that was very real to me. I was in an accident and my Range Rover was rolling down to a valley. I woke up while shaking and sweating. I looked at the boys and said to myself that I should not take them with me. The following morning I spoke to my father and asked him that I wanted to send my sons and the servant back to Iran by plane. My father yelled at me that I was out of my mind; that I was driving a car and had plenty of room for all of them but I would waste the money just because I had a silly dream. I had the same dreams for the next few nights. Therefore I decided to take the boys, my little niece and the servant to the airport and send them back home by plane. I woke up very early before anybody was up and took them to the airport. When I returned and my father found out what I did, he was really mad at me and slapped me. I cried and said if I had an accident I could die but my children would be safe. So we started on our journey.

I was at the front and my two brothers were following me. Even though the car already had its first service I felt that there was something wrong with it. When we arrived in Germany, I took the car to a Range Rover garage and asked them to check it out for my peace of mind. They checked everything and said that there was nothing wrong with that. We continued with our journey. We camped in most countries in Europe and had a lovely time. At that time Turkey invaded Cyprus, therefore we could not get to Turkey. We were forced to stay in a little village in Greece until the border with Turkey was reopened. When we've got to the Turkish border, the head of the border patrol wanted £1,000 for each car to allow us to pass the border. And this time my father was not with us and we did not carry that much cash. I told them that we were students and we did not have that sort of money. He said he would take one of our cars otherwise we would not be moving anywhere. I could understand Turkish and I was the only one that he was talking to. They put us aside with an armed soldier watching us. We had to sleep inside the cars that night. I could not sleep even for a minute, since a couple of the officers kept moving around my car and doing revolting things; it was a horrible night. At midnight, I realised a car came with lots of illegal merchandise and the border officers emptied it. I took the car's number plate and I recognised the driver as we talked with him while we were waiting at the border. He gave us his home address and phone number and said when we got to Istanbul, we should look him up. In the morning I went to the office and talked to the officer in charge. I told him in Turkish that I saw what happened last night. I said I would leave our cars to go to the Consulate and report them as I had all the information, including the driver's name and address. First he thought that I was bluffing but when I showed him the address and phone number he went silent and got cranky, swearing and yelled at the soldier to let us go. We stayed in hotels a couple of nights and then continued going toward Iran. On the way we stopped at a café and I said I felt a bit tired. My sister-in-law offered to come and join me in my car. As we were driving through the mountains, it was a very winding and rough road. A truck in front of me was causing a lot of dust and made it hard for me to see properly. I tried to overtake him but every time I tried he blocked me. He was doing that on purpose as he could see our number plates and knew we were tourists. On one bend I decided to overtake him again but all of a sudden I felt that the steering wheel was out of my control. I rolled over with the Range Rover down into a very deep valley. The minute I felt out of control the only thing I remember was saying "Allah".

My brother who was behind me said that my sister-in-law was thrown out of the window on the first roll and after a couple of rolls the front window came out and I was thrown out of the car. Lots of village people, instead of helping, started stealing our belongings until my middle brother started to yell and also a bus full of Iranian students stopped to give us assistance. My oldest brother was in a shock; he was not able to do anything. The bus driver, who was a Turkish man, helped to bring me out of the valley. By then I opened my eyes and asked for some water. As my brother was giving me the water, the Turkish driver stopped him, saying that I would die if I drank the water. He put us all in my oldest brother's car and took us to a hospital in the village. We got to the hospital that was very primitive and had not any doctors or nurses. One of the workers put staples on my cuts and then when they put me in the hospital bed, I had my first "out-of-body" experience. I was in the air, watching my body on the bed. I could see all the hospital patients around the bed and my family who were all crying, screaming and praying. I felt no pain; I was very peaceful and talking to God. All I could see was lots of bright and glowing light. I said to God that I was happy if he wanted to take me but asked him if there was anybody to look after my two boys. That was the only thing I was worried about. I looked down and I could see my two boys crying and calling me. Then suddenly I dropped back into my body. And then I was screaming from pain. My sister-in-law had an injury on top of her knee and was in extreme shock. She was in the next bed to me. They got in touch with the doctor who came the following day, and they X rayed both of us to check for any broken bones. My sister-in-law did not have any but I had fractured jaw and a fractured hipbone. I also lost my upper front teeth. The doctor suggested that we should be taken back to Iran and be treated there. They put me on one piece of wood, strapped me to it so that I would not move and put me in the back of the truck. The doctor gave both of us very strong painkillers and as we arrived to the border the whole family was already waiting there. My father also came to the hospital in Turkey; they told him that we just left so he followed us to Iran. My brother arranged for the Range Rover to be brought back to England as the police in Turkey reported that faulty axles caused the accident.

We were taken to hospital, which was just on the border, and stayed there during the night. The doctors there cleaned out our wounds and did further tests and they realise that my right knee was full of sand and glass, which they had to clean out and dress. My sister-in-law's mother and sister were all the time around her and were blaming me for the accident but my sister-in-law, an earthy angel, was crying for me and saying not to worry. I was very upset for what happened to her but obviously it was another God's plan for her to be in my car during the last part of our journey. The next day we were sent to Tehran and I stayed with my mother because the doctor said that I should be resting on a wooden bed and not to move at all. So they provided a special bed for me. That was for my broken hip; they said when I've got better, they could start and operate on my other injuries as they were not life threatening and could therefore wait until I was better. I was in a lot of pain and upset because of my injuries, especially the injury to my face. They put me on lots of strong painkillers, sleeping tablets and tranquillizers. I had to send my sons with the servant to their father who was living with his parents at that time, as my mother was not willing to look after me as well as my sons. My mother loved her privacy, comfort and freedom. Therefore she was constantly complaining to me that I had spoiled her plans. She had to put a bedpan for me that she did not appreciate and she was supposed to clean me up which she did not do. My mother still had a cleaning lady, who come in to do the housework but she did not have anybody to live with her permanently. She also asked my father to pay for all my expenses otherwise she would not look after me. When my father came to visit me he said that he lost a lot of money over this accident but he did not care about it and was happy that I am alive. He said he would support me until I get better but after that I was on my own. He said that he had a wife and his own life to live and cannot support me any longer.

My mother was very close to her neighbour who had two young sons and they had full access to my mother's home. On a couple of occasions my mother would go out at night and would ask one of the neighbour's sons to come and stay with me. One of the boys was 21 and the other 19 and they both would take turns staying with me. I found out that both of them fell in love with me even though they knew I was married. I had to be very diplomatic with them as they were young boys with a lot of passion. One day their mother came and asked me what I was trying to do to her boys. I responded I am sick and lying in this bed. I did not encourage them at all. She replied that they were fighting over me and asked me for help. I said that when I get better, I will talk to them and begged her not to agree to send them over to take care of me anymore. It was my mother's selfishness that caused all that. I mentioned to my mother what happened but she just laughed at me and said that I was out of my mind. She asked me if I looked in the mirror lately and saw how I looked now.

One night while I was asleep I felt things crawling all over me and when I felt them on my face I screamed. My mother woke up, put the light on and we found thousands of big cockroaches all over me. From that night on, I did not sleep. I had the light on and I would read or write poems. I would sleep in the morning. I told the doctor, who would come and visit me regularly, about this incident. He said that I needed to be kept clean at all times otherwise these things would happen. So he suggested that we get a bottle of pure alcohol from the pharmacy and wash my whole body with the alcohol. When one of my aunties came to visit me, my mother asked her to wash me. After six weeks I was able to walk slowly with two crutches but my knee was swollen and hurting all the time. They took couple of X-rays but they could not find anything wrong. I just had to cope with the excruciating pain and take pain killer all the time. I went to the dentist and he fixed all my front teeth.

My husband used to come and visit me every fortnight but he was not supportive or caring at all. He was a very suspicious man. He didn't trust anyone and had hardly any friends. He didn't even trust his own family. Even on our arrival to the border he did not treat me nicely, my accident was like a huge inconvenience to him. I'd already decided to divorce him, as he was horrible to me during the time when I needed him most and I saw no point to start a life with a man who was treating me badly from the beginning.

My father stopped supporting me and my mother asked me to leave. I did O level English and 3 A levels through London Board University; then I went to Birmingham University and did one year engineering which my dad wanted. I had to stop studying due to my accident and several operations. I went to my first husband's parents who were looking after my children at that time and asked them to allow me to stay there until I could find some other accommodation for my sons and myself. By this time my first husband had gone to America to continue with his studies. They refused to help me. I could not continue with my studies and asked my mother to give me time to find a job and a place to live. I asked my father if he would help me but he also refused. By this time my father had all his finances under his own control. I said to my parents "What am I suppose to do? Live in a street?" And they both responded, "We don't care!"

I went to see one of my second cousins who was a very famous singer. I explained my situation and asked her to help me to become a singer. I had a very nice and strong voice and I had done a lot of performances since childhood. She sent me to her cousin who was a famous composer and after auditioning, he said I had a very good future and he had couple of songs ready for me. He took me to a recording studio and we recorded couple of songs, then I had a contract with a music company. We also recorded a video clip in way of promotion but the composer fell in love with me madly and wanted to marry me. I did not want to as he was on drugs. However, I admitted his love that made him protective of me in that environment.

One night when I went to my mother's house she would not let me in. She said that she did not care where I went but I could not come to her home any more. I slept in the car until the morning and then she let me in. I told her that the composer wanted to go to England with me to bring a whole music studio and some antiques to sell. He would put up the money and I would use my status in England to export the goods to Iran. At the time, the law was when you lived in England and wanted to go back to your home country, you could take your household furniture and belongings without any custom. Our arrangement was that he would keep the music studio and I would keep all the household goods. Then we would sell all the antiques and divide the profit in half. My mother agreed and she would like to come with us as we were going by car. She wanted to see her sons again in England, as well. We left Iran and went to England. During our stay in England I contacted British Leyland's manager and informed them of my accident regarding the faulty Range Rover. They were aware of the accident as they'd already had the car there. They offered to give me a replacement car plus £20,000 compensation for my injuries. I did not accept this offer and went to see our solicitor regarding my rights. The solicitor advised me that I should be able to get at least £1,000,000 in compensation for all my pain and suffering. I left the case with him but I went back to Iran and then due to the revolution, I could not return to England to pursue the case. After 2 years my brother advised me that the case was dismissed. To this day I do not understand how this could have happened; I believe that the British Leyland bribed my solicitor. While we were in England we stayed in my father's house and it was so inconvenient because my stepmother and mother were constantly clashing and I had to keep the peace. We were there for two months and we bought all the goods and put them on a 10 tonne container to be shipped back to Iran. We left the car in England with my father and we flew back to Iran. I stayed at the musician's house as a business arrangement because I did not trust him as he had a drug problem. I had no other choices at the time, too. He gave up his addiction before our trip and when we came back he would go back to his bad habits. We received all the goods back in Iran and started to sell some of the antiques; then I got some money.

I made some inquiries to continue my studies. I always wanted to become a skin specialist and cosmetologist. I found a private institute, which was connected to the Tehran University and also a University of Beauty in Paris. I started to study while I was still living with the musician. He used to sleep until about 2 pm and would not go to bed until about 4 am. He supported me in my studies and was proud of my ability and strength to continue despite all my setbacks. I continued my study and finally became skin specialist.

At the time my children were still living with their grandparents and our servant who was looking after them. My heart was in pain every moment since I could not be with my children but I had no other choices. That was why I was studying so hard to be eventually able to look after my sons and myself. I used to spend time with them during weekends.

One day I had a phone call from my children's auntie to inform me that my oldest son, who was 7 years old at the time, fell into their empty swimming pool which was about 3 meters deep and fractured his skull and that he was taken to a hospital. I ran to the hospital; when I saw my son, I fainted myself. They brought me back and I looked at my son whose head was so swollen that you could not see his eyes. He could not talk or move but when I held his hand he moved his head towards me. I bent on my knees and prayed to God to save my son's life and I made a promise to God that I will look after the needs of 10 orphan boys; and also on his birthday I will give money and food and other needs to 50 poor families every year. (In Islam we do offerings to the poor while we pray and we call it "Nazr"). The doctor said "What are you praying for? You are an educated woman, you should know better and pray to God to take him and stop him from suffering." He had a haemorrhage on his brain and even if he would survive, he would be disabled and they could do nothing at all for him. I did not listen to them since I believed in God more than them. Their father was in America and none of his family was in the hospital. They took my son to the hospital and then just left. The hospital said I couldn't move him anywhere unless another doctor was in charge. I called one of my old family friends who was a neurosurgeon and explained what had happened. He came immediately to the hospital and told me that we would take him to his home and if my son still was alive by the morning then he would start treating him. But he said nothing can be done before then unless he should not go to sleep otherwise he was gone. He also was a believer in God's miracle. My friend released my son from the hospital and took us to his place. When we arrived his wife was very welcoming and understanding. She gave us a room. We put my son in the bed and I sat next to him and was constantly talking to him so that he would not go to sleep. It was 6 o'clock in the morning and my son was alive. I screamed and called the doctor "He is alive! He is alive!" He came and we immediately went to his hospital. He started to treat my son with and put him on a drip to feed him intravenously. It took couple of weeks until my son was able to function normally but he had a big fracture on his skull running from just above his eyebrow to the back of his head. He was also on a lot of medication and had to be checked up regularly by a neurologist.

They told me that even though he has passed the danger, he would not be able to perform academically and we had to be very careful with his daily activity. So I had to watch him all the time and be worry about him in case he bumps his head. We had a couple of incidents when he was playing with other children; he would pass out and he would have a concussion that I had to take him to hospital again to be treated. This went on for seven years with some abnormalities and he used to get a lot of headaches and bloodshot eyes. We were advised that he should avoid any stress or get angry and upset but despite all this, he still went to school, performed reasonably well and finished his degree with honours. He is married with two beautiful children, *another miracle of God.*

The musician's brother had a 2-bedroom apartment, which I was able to rent. I was so happy that I could take my children with me after one year of separation. But the musician would still come and go to the house and was causing me lots of heartache. I'd already learnt about skin treatment such as facial and makeup. I also had hairdressing diploma and learnt hair removal treatment. Therefore I made one of the rooms into a hair and beauty salon and lived in the other room. I managed to study, work from home and look after my children even though my health was not good (I learned to live with my sick body). The musician kept asking me to marry him. As I was refusing, he started to become nasty and on some occasions he would bring his friends at midnight, stay there until the morning and smoking drugs. Therefore I thought that I had to move and I never let my boys see him while doing that and bringing strangers to the house. I started to have fear for my own and my children's safety, as well. All my family was overseas and my mother did not care. So I went to one of my uncles and explain my situation to him and I asked to tell his 20 years old son to come and stay with us for a while until I could organise a new place to stay. Therefore he came and stayed with us but the musician got even nastier because my cousin stood up to him and said he could not behave this way anymore or bring any strangers.

The musician went and made a false statement to the Islamic Republic organisation, "the comity". The statement was that I brought different men to the house; he also managed to get the form signed by the tenants from the block where I was living. It was evening when an armed comity man knocked on the door and informed me of the accusations. I started to cry and said it was a total lie. I explained that the musician was a drug addict and I was a hard working mother with two children and that he has been harassing me for a long time. But it did not matter what I said as he did not believe me. He looked at me and said he would give me 48 hours to think about two options: He would marry me to save me. He had lots of money and houses and could give me a nice house and would look after me and my children. He said that my other option was to be put in jail to be punished. My children would be given to a family or orphanage. After he left, I was devastated. The only person who could save me from this situation was my second husband who was still in contact with me as a friend. He used to say if I ever needed his help, he would help me with pleasure and if I gave him another chance, he would never mistreat me. Therefore I decided to go to his parents' house, as he was still living with them, to ask for his help.

I had a car, which was one of the Princesses that my father gave me. When I got there with my children, while I was crying, I told the whole family my story and asked him "If you want me, I am ready to marry you". This was the only way we could be safe from the comity man. The family celebrated and he was also very happy.

I stayed there overnight with the children. The next morning we went to the registry office and got married for the second time. We went to my house with his family and packed all my belongings and left all the antiques in the house for the musician. After the 48 hours the comity man knocked on the door and as I opened the door he asked me about my decision. I said I let my husband talk to him. He replied "Don't talk nonsense." My husband said Hello to him but he still did not believe it and accused my husband of being one of my lovers. My husband told him to watch his language and showed our marriage certificate. Then the comity man went silent and gave me a dirty look and left very unhappy. I rang my mother, who was in England at the time, to ask if we could move into her house that was in north Tehran for one month. We moved out of the musician's brother's house and went to my mother's house. My children and I were very happy. We thought that we were finally going to have a stable family environment.

My second husband was so good, caring and kind. He was a totally changed man from the one I left previously which made me fall in love with him. After a month we found a big house which was divided into two separate but connected units and had a big back yard, swimming pool and also the second access from another street. I set up my clinic in one of the units and we lived in the other one. By this time I'd already completed my degree in skin and beauty specialist and had an established clientele. I was the breadwinner in our family as my husband's wages would be enough just for his personal expenses. But he was a high army officer and also a very good handy man who would fix things for me but he would not help with any housework. His believed if a man does any housework, even just making a cup of tea, he is not a real man. He begged me to have a child, as he would love to have a child with me. So, soon after I became pregnant and it was the worst pregnancy I had. I was constantly vomiting. I was living on just some apples and dry bread. I started to bleed about 4 months into the pregnancy as well, which was due to all my previous health problems. I was 28 years old and I thought that I was too old to have a baby. Within four months, my husband went back to his original personality, even worse. He started bringing up all the past events and calling me with horrible names. I just said to God "I thought you sent me and my children a saviour but all the suffering started again". I tried to ignore the hurtful things he was saying and just continue working, looking after the family and coping with my health problems. He was never supporting me; in fact he would not even believe me. The only time he paid some attention was when I was bleeding and he had to take me to hospital or call the doctor home. The doctor was saying that my bleeding was related to too much work and too much stress but no one cared. One night when I was asleep he woke me up and started questioning me about my intimate relationship with my first husband. I told him that we were husband and wife and we had two children. I asked him why he would ask these questions then. He started to shake me and said, "Answer me!" I cried and said, "I hate all men. Intimacy never had any meaning for me. All I wanted was to find a man who would be loving and caring and compassionate. The way you were when we got married for the second time I thought you are going to be the one; but now you are torturing me. All that should matter is that I am your wife, I am carrying your baby and I want to live with you peacefully". But he replied he was constantly thinking about my past relationships. He thought I had slept with many men and he could not let it go. As the time went on he became worse. He started to be very strict to the stage that if he would come home and see his younger brother visiting us, he would throw him out and said "Don't you dare come here while I am not at home". And then he would ask me if I slept with him. So, none of his brothers or his father was allowed to come when he was not at home. I said he needed to see a doctor because he had a kind of mental disorder. But he believed I wanted to put a label on him to be able to do all my dirty jobs! His mother was a very nice lady, very loving and caring and I knew her from my childhood. She was always on my side and telling him off for treating me the way he was.

When the Islamic Republic took over the King's government, they were forcing lots of Islamic rules onto people. One of them was that all women should be covered from head to toe and also not allowed to wear any make up or nail polish in public. They announced if there is anyone who would like to protest against the decision, she could gather together to express their opinion against this decision. Millions of women from all over the country met together in the middle of all large cities. Tehran had the highest number of women attending. My mother and many relatives and friends and I attended that rally. All we did was to march peacefully and present our opinion regarding the "cover up" rule. Within a very short time a group of women appeared who were totally covered in black outfits from head to toe (chador). They all were armed with knives and blades. They started throwing stones at us and attacked all the women who were protesting against. Within few moments lots of women were injured, bleeding and screaming and the rest started to run away as fast as they could. So, the next day, they announced there were more women in the country who agree to be covered up and not wear any make up. From then on it would be compulsory to obey this rule and anyone not complying with this rule would be prosecuted and jailed. I was totally against this rule but I had no choice and had to wear the chador and not have any make up or nail polish on.

I had a phone call from my father to inform me that my middle brother, who was always in trouble, was going to come back to Iran after about eight years living in England. We went and picked him up from the airport. He was supposed to live with my mother who was living in a big house by herself. So, she had a party for him and he stayed with her. One week later, my mother rang and told me that she kicked my brother out of her house. She wanted me to go and pick him up. When we got there my brother was so angry, yelling and swearing at my mother outside her house. I had to calm him down and brought him to my house as my mother would not give up her comfort and privacy for anyone, not even her own children.

Therefore, I had to give him one of the rooms in my clinic. It was not very convenient but I could not desert him because I loved him. My mother rang again and said that I didn't have to look after him. She believed that he is old enough to look after himself. Because of this, my mother would not come to my house for a while. In the meantime, I was trying to calm my brother down to accept our mother as she was. My brother had a diploma in auto mechanics therefore, after a couple of months, he started to work. Meanwhile, before working, he was having fun; going out with different girls secretly as it was a crime in Iran. I kept warning him that if he got caught he would be punished. He would still drink alcohol, which was illegal as well, and he was a heavy smoker. He all the time would have some friends or relatives with him. I had to constantly serve him and all his male guests. We did not even know some of these people; they were somebody he just met. This behaviour was causing even more problems between my husband and me but my husband would never show his anger in front of my brother. Instead, he would take it out on me in private.

As he was doing all these crazy things, he decided to move to one of my father's apartments to have more space and opportunities. Within a week I had a phone call from comity informing me that my brother was in jail and if I could go and bail him out. Prior to that, he had disappeared for 3 days and when I asked the neighbours in the building they told me that he was taken by comity due to his behaviour. My husband and I looked for him in every comity centre but we could not find him. I was very happy to hear about him. We immediately went there and brought him back home. He was so scared and he cried in my arms. So I took him home and he explained that he was punished by comity. That experience really frightened him and he promised that he would behave.

When I was 28 weeks pregnant, I dreamt that I gave birth to a little girl who was very tiny. I saw Mary and Fatima and handed the baby to them and said she is too tiny to survive. They gave her back to me and said she is a very special little girl. I have to look after her by myself and she will be fine. The next morning, I told my husband, my mother and my mother-in-law about my dream. Everyone made fun of me. The next day, I went for my monthly check up. As soon as the doctor checked me, she said to my husband that I was ready to have my baby. As the baby was premature, she had to give me some injection so that if the baby was born the lungs would develop. Within two days, I was in labour and had the baby. The baby was put into incubator and they also told me that she had jaundice; within a day she had some infection as well. I left the hospital without my daughter and went home. I had lots of milk and was very uncomfortable and it was a very painful period in my life to go home without my baby. I used to call the hospital every two hours and visit her every day. I could only watch her from behind the glass. Every time they gave me bad news. Within five days, they rang and informed me that I should come and see the baby for the last time, as they did not think she would survive another day. I went to the hospital and told the doctors that I would like to take my baby home. If she was going to die, she would die in my arms. They were totally against this but they could not go against my decision. So, they took her out of the incubator and disconnected all the tubes. I could not even put any clothes on her; I just had to wrap her in a piece of soft material. She was 1.6 kg and 48 cm long; she was just skin and bone. Even though she did not look like a normal baby, as she had no fat on her body, but to me she was the most beautiful baby in the world. I remembered about my dream; when I saw the baby who was so tiny, I gave her to Fatima and Marry and told them she was so tiny and would die. But they gave me the baby back and said "look after her; she will be fine as she is very special". The baby had no voice and looked like an old lady in a little body. It would take me two hours to breast feed her as she had no strength to suck; one suck and rest for a while! I sterilized the house and didn't have any visitors, except close family. I didn't move from her side for two months; just prayed all the time and checked if she was breathing. During that time, she didn't have a name. Whatever names I thought about or heard didn't suit her. After two months, a name was given to me whom I had never heard of. I just called her the name! My husband said "It's a nice name. Where did it came from?" and I answered I didn't know. At the time, she was 4.5 kg, healthy and so beautiful, ***another miracle of God***.

My father ended up losing his trust toward his second wife and they had lots of problems until finally they divorced and she came back to Iran. My father made a phone call and asked me to change the lock and to make sure that she could not go to his apartment. I disagreed but he yelled at me and told me to do as his order. Therefore, I changed the lock. When she tried to get in she could not; she went to police and court and managed to get access to the apartment. I was happy with that decision and I was not responsible for what happened as I did what my father asked. I went to visit her and the children but she was very nasty with me and did not let me hold my stepbrothers. She asked me to leave and said all of us were going to be sorry for what we did to her. I responded that I only followed my father's orders. She lived in an apartment in my father's building.

My father sent me an authority for all his assets and I used to go to collect rents monthly from the 16 apartments, 14 shops and a factory that my father owned. About a couple of months after, my father came back to Iran. He was not well. He had stiffness all over his body due to high triglycerides that he ended up in bed and I ended up looking after him as well as my three children and my husband. Within a week of his arrival my step mother came to the house and yelled that since I was looking after him, I should look after his two boys. She left the boys who were then 18 and 9 months old. So, I ended up looking after 5 children, the youngest being just 40 days and the oldest 9 years old. My stepbrothers were calling me "mum" and I even breastfed my youngest stepbrother. When my stepmother came for a visit and they would call her by her given name, she would become even angrier. She believed that I was interfering in her life. If I wouldn't take care of my father and his sons he would be back with her. It did not matter what I did for anybody I always ended up being blamed.

On top of all the responsibilities of looking after my father, my own children and my step brothers, there were also all the visitors who came to see my father to look after. On many occasions my stepmother would come for a visit and would end up with a big fight and argument between her and my father. That used to always worry me and I tried very hard to defuse the situation.

My husband's only sister used to come to our house all the time and even helped me; she liked my brother, I liked her as well. I said to my brother on a couple of occasions that he should marry her and she would be a good wife for him. But he always made fun and ignored the subject. When he came out of jail, he said that I was right and he should get married to her and settles down. I was very happy and informed my mother about it. Her family was quite happy and we had a wedding for them; they started their life in that one room in my clinic. Soon after the wedding, his wife was pregnant and within two months of pregnancy she changed to a totally different person. She stopped helping me with the housework and she did not care about anybody else. On a couple of occasions, in front of everyone, she insulted me and my brother calling us bad names exactly like her brother. On one occasion as she was very rude to me, one of her brothers told her to be quiet and appreciate all the things that I had done to her. She insulted him as well. He slapped her across the mouth and she started to bleed from her mouth but she did not stop swearing. As he went to hit her again, I jumped in the middle, grabbed her and pushed her inside her room and closed the door. I asked her to be quiet otherwise he would kill her. She did not stop. She continued yelling and swearing. The rest of the family were watching. I asked everybody to just please leave and she would calm down later on. My brother was very upset after this occasion to the degree that he wanted to get divorce but I persuaded him against it. I said that I would arrange for one of the apartments that our father owned to be cleared out and he and his wife could move there.

It would give them privacy and things should settle down. They moved out to their new place and I also arranged and paid for all the furniture they needed. But they still continued to have arguments throughout their married life

When my father got better, he decided to collect the rental fees by himself. I disagreed and told him that he should stay away as his ex-wife was living there and could cause trouble for him. But he didn't accept that. So, he went and took his 2 youngest sons with him. After finishing the job and while he was leaving the building, my stepmother came in front of him and as usual started to yell and swear at him. As she could not provoke him, she started to hit him. My father pushed her out of his way and the next thing the comity arrived and handcuffed him and took him away. One of the tenants rang and informed me that my father had been taken away. I was very upset but I could not do anything. Within an hour, my stepmother came to my house with 6 armed comity men. At the time, I was giving a bath to my little girl. When I looked through the "peep hole," I saw them. It terrified me. I had my right leg in a plaster due to a broken ankle that was happened a couple of weeks earlier. I ran to the other access in the back yard and I started to yell to all the neighbours to help me as I was by myself. The armed men came round to the other street access where I was and started to shoot into the air and yell at everybody in the neighbourhood and tell them to go to their home and to shut their eyes and mouths; then they pushed me inside the house. My daughter was crying so I asked them to allow me to pick up my baby. I wrapped the baby in a towel and dressed her while one of the armed men was pointing his machinegun at me. They asked me to cover up my hair which I did. They pushed me with the baby into a corner of the room. Then they started to search the whole house, looking for some evidence to destroy the whole family; because my step mother had told them we had drugs and also we were against the government. I begged my stepmother, who was leading the comity to stay, that I was very scared but she ignored and left me with all these armed men.

One man out of the six, I believed, was sent by God to protect my daughter and me. He was the one constantly asked the others to stop being rude and nasty to me as they still did not have any evidence against me. They totally trashed my whole house looking for any evidence. Meanwhile, one of the neighbours contacted my husband and explained the situation to him. My husband rang the house but one of the comity men answered the phone and did not allow me to talk to him. My husband contacted my brothers and my mother so everyone arrived within one hour and after about 6 hours of distress they found a piece of paper that had some insulting writing about the Islamic government that was planted there by my step mother. Luckily, the note was not hand written but typed and therefore they could not prove who did it. When they showed it to me I swore on Koran and my children's life that I had never seen that paper before. But they did not believe me. My husband had to leave and go back to work immediately as he was ordered to do so by his supervisors. The comity took videos, music tapes and some of our photo albums containing photos of us on holidays in swimming costumes as evidence against us. They took my two brothers and me to their centre. When we got there, they started to question us separately. They said because of the typed note which they found in my house, they would take us all to the centre of the town and shoot us. I answered, as I did before, that I had never seen that piece of paper in my life and I have no idea where it came from. They were very rude, aggressive and abusive. After questioning us for hours, they let us go home, however, I had to go to the comity centre every day for further questioning. My oldest brother was just back from England due to his belief, as a very strong Muslim, to serve the Islamic government. Both my oldest brother and I never missed a prayer or fasting and I used to read Koran and knew most of the verses by heart but according to comity we were not true Muslims.

When I got back home, my two sons were very upset and terrified but they were happy to see me back. The comity took over my father's building and all the tenants had to give the rent money to comity. My father was kept in jail and tortured. A man who was in his cell rang us and asked for helping our father before they kill him. But we could do nothing. I had to go every day to the comity centre and be questioned by the comity man while he was hitting my forehead with his gun and frightening me. My husband would come with our daughter. He told them that by the Islamic rule he should be in the room and it is not right that his wife questioned by a man alone. He told my husband that I was old enough and if he talked too much, they would not allow him to come and wait outside the room for me. For 30 days I had to report there and be asked the same questions over and over again. After about 2 weeks, I had a phone call from comity telling me to go to the centre where my father was kept and send all those people who were protesting against my father's imprisonment back home. The comity accused me of bribing these people to go and protest against them. I went there to see who they were. For the first time, I saw all those people who my father had been supporting for years without anybody's knowledge. They were demanding their monthly payment, which they used to receive from my father's accountant. That day they allowed me to visit my father for the first time. He was in a terrible shape, and he was so happy to see me as the nasty comity has been telling him that I was in another cell and that they were "fixing" me up. About two weeks after this, they took my father to court and we all went to court, too. My stepmother was there with her two boys, as well. My father was brought to court in handcuffs. The two little boys cried and wanted to run to my father and me but she grabbed them and pulled them away from us. They gave two years jail sentence to my father for domestic violence against my stepmother. We were crying and she was laughing!

They put my father into government jail and I used to visit him once a week, which was not pleasant at all. I had to stay in a queue for about 3-4 hours to visit him for 10-15 minutes behind bars. The contact could only be by the phone. Even in jail, he wanted to help poor people so therefore every time he would give me somebody's name and address to deliver food, money and whatever they needed. Because of that, all the prisoners loved him and were looking after him. For that reason they kept changing his jail. He was in 4 different jails during his 2 years and some were 4 hours drive away from Tehran. I never missed a week visiting him even with all the responsibilities I had. During some visitations, he would be yelling and swearing at me for no reason as he was under a lot of pressure. My two oldest brothers only visited him twice in two years because they could not cope with his changed behaviour. I went to the Minister of the Islamic Government and complained about the trauma affected my family and me, for no apparent reason. They did some investigation and apologised by a letter. They released my father building to me, but my father had to go through his jail sentence. Therefore, I arranged for three other apartments on the first floor to be cleared out. I took two of them—one to live in and one for work and the other one I gave to my oldest brother. Later on, I gave one of the units to my mother as well, since she was not feeling safe to live by herself as she was robbed a couple of times. The whole family were living in the one building, again. There were always problems amongst them and I was the problem solver, not just my own family but also the relatives, i.e. cousins, uncles, aunties. My house was like a refuge centre because I always welcomed everybody. My mother's family had always problems amongst them. You would never see the six sisters and brothers together at a family function. The only function they all attended was my first wedding. After about six months, my mother decided to move out to a big house. My mother sponsored about four girls and boys from an orphanage, which used to belong to the Queen. As the Islamic government took over, all the orphanages were closed down and the children needed to go to homes. One of those kids (a girl) who was abandoned by her mother, because the baby lost her feet in a fire, didn't find any parents. Therefore, my mother had to take her home. By that time, the girl was about 18 years old and had finished her high school education. We used to see these kids every weekend and acknowledge them as our sisters and brothers. One day, my mother rang me and said that she kicked the girl out of the house. She was outside the house, screaming and crying. My mother said that she could not handle her and wanted me to take her. I went there and found her crying. She said my mother wanted to treat her as a servant not as an adopted daughter. They had so many arguments and it was impossible for them to live together. She wanted love and warmth from my mother but my mother did not know how to even give that to her own children. I had to take her home and look after her. I did not have a spare room, so she had to sleep in the living room but I gave her all the love and caring she was seeking. I encouraged her to study and opposite to my mother, who used to put her down, I gave her confidence and self-esteem regardless of her physical disability. She studied nursing and met a nice boy during her studies. He also had orphanage background and they got married and have two beautiful children. They still live in Tehran but she had no more contact with my mother.

My father was released from jail after he served his two-year sentence and he came to live with me. I used to have my two little half brothers with me as they were living in the same building with their mother. But I had no contact with their mother. When my father started living with me, she started to come around again but my oldest son threw her out. Therefore she changed her plan as she wanted my father back. Every time she got my father outside the building, she would cry and beg him for forgiveness. And she would again send her sons to my place every day for me to look after them. I could not trust her but on some occasions, when my boys were not at home, she would come to my place and I could not throw her out because of my personality.

I always was catering for the whole family but finally I started to have lots of problems, more than ever, with them. My health was deteriorating. I had to have another operation, which was during the Iran/Iraq war, and I almost died. After 15 days I came out of hospital, continually suffering with pain and infection. After a year, another surgeon found out that some of the internal stiches were not removed. That was the reason of my constant pain and infection and I had to have another operation to remove the cause. The only rest I was getting in my life was when I was in a hospital bed. My second son also had lots of digestive problems. He was crying and complaining of constant stomach pain. That was going on for also about a year and finally after so many different visits to specialists it was fixed. One day my daughter's youngest uncle took her for a walk in her pram. They came back home and my daughter was in a deep sleep. Apparently, while he was pushing the pram over a bump, she was thrown out of the pram and fell onto the concrete. Therefore she went to this heavy sleep that lasted for about three days. I could just wake her up for her feed and she would go back to sleep again. The uncle was scared to tell us what happened but I could see he was very worried because he kept asking about her. After three days he confessed to what happened, as he was worried. Therefore I took her to hospital and had her checked up and the result was good. The doctors said she had a concussion. Up to the age of 14 she was very sensitive to any even slight movement as she would vomit. Beside that there were lots of fights and arguments amongst my 2 brothers and my father. I got shingles from one of my patients without knowing that she had it. It was very painful and I was treating it but it was a very slow process. Dealing with all the difficulties plus my sickness, I was desperate for some help. So, one day I went to a very spiritual holy lady who was nearly 100 years old but glowing with a beautiful aura. She was serving God all her life and never married. I asked her for help because I felt there was something in my house that was causing so much sickness and problems. She said "There is a woman in your family who has put some black magic into your whole house and wants you dead." She gave me some special prayer to carry with and also put it under my pillow. She also taught me how to make holy water using prayer and the Koran and she told me to pour the holy water over my wound. At the time it shocked me because I did not believe in the existence of black magic. She advised me to search my house and I would find it. When I got home, I searched the whole house with the help of my two sons and my sister-in-law and we found five pieces of paper that had some writing emphasising all the things that were happening in our family including a message that I should be dead. So, after that I did believe what the old lady told me. My oldest son told my stepmother off and told her never to come to this door again; he called her "wicked witch". After we cleared the house, the household was more peaceful with just usual problems. I also used the holy water on my wound and the next day the wound disappeared. By this time my father was again involved with my stepmother. She was acting totally opposite to her previous behaviour and was playing on my father's feelings with emotional blackmail. My heart broke when I found out about their involvement again. I told my father how he could accept her again after all she had done to him and his family. But he said, "I am worried about those two little boys' future. They need their father's support. But I am not going to live with her or trust her ever again." About a year after that, my father decided to buy a 10-acre holiday house at a seaside, which was about four hours drive from Tehran. He built a mansion on the property and was hoping to get all his children transfer there as well, since he was ashamed of all the disasters that happened to him and his family. We would go there just during the holidays and he used to come occasionally to stay with me. But my stepmother started to go with the boys and stay. That ended up living there with him but he never re-married her. When I found it out, that really devastated me regardless of his reason. I knew deep down that it was not going to have a good ending.

My father died of a massive heart attack in 1998. During the 12 years of living with my stepmother, he never trusted her; not even eating food that was cooked by her. They had lots of problems and the poor two little boys suffered the most by this situation.

One day my oldest son broke his hip while was playing. He had to lie on a hard surface for six weeks. He was not allowed to move until the fracture healed. It was very difficult on top of all my other responsibilities to take care of him which I did it with all my heart. He was very attached to me since his last accident when he fractured his skull.

When the Islamic Republic took over Iran, they acknowledged only a few religions such as Christianity, Judaism and Zoroastrianism; but none of the other religions like Buddhism, Hindu, Baha'i (Baha'i religion originated in Iran over hundred years ago) etc were allowed. My grandfather was a very devoted Muslim who converted to Baha'i after the birth of my mother. However, even though my grandmother had to convert to Baha'i, she never accepted it and was still practising Islam in secret. My mother's first marriage was to a Baha'i man and one of my aunties was also married to a Baha'i. After my grandfather's death, the rest of his family converted back to Islam. My half sister was brought up by a Baha'i father and also married a Baha'i man, so she is a devoted Baha'i. The Islamic government started to cause lots of trouble for them and they were all terrified. My sister and her family had to sell their house and escape the country. In the meantime, they had to live somewhere before they made the arrangement to get out of the country, as they could not leave the country being Baha'i. The only way was to escape or convert to Islam. I welcomed her and her family into my house but my mother did not support them; in fact she caused them so many problems as they were staying with me. After a month, they had to move to one of my aunties for a while and then they left the country and migrated to another country.

I was praying during the month of Muslim fasting (Ramadan) while I was sick and having lots of problems. My husband would come to the room and start insulting me by saying "You cannot cover your sins with fasting and praying to God". This would really hurt me. I continued praying and ask for God's help. I was begging God to save me from this situation, as I could not take it any longer. Sometimes I used to pray and ask God "take me if you cannot save me." It was our New Year and my father said that we could go to Australia to visit my auntie (my mother's sister—the mother of my cousins that was killed in the bike accident with my brother). My father always loved her like a daughter and I also had very close connection with her. Therefore we contacted them and they were also very happy to see us. We went to the Australian Embassy and applied for tourist visa but unfortunately our application was declined. We informed our auntie and she even arrange some invitation but it still made no difference. I gave up and continued to pray to be saved. I opened the Koran to receive a message about my situation, while I was praying. There was a miraculous story, which was indicating a miracle is going to happen to save me. Five months later I decided to go to the Australian Embassy and try it again. Usually there was a long queue of people waiting for different visas, but when I got to the Australian Embassy, I did not see anyone outside. When I got inside, a man who was a clerk came toward me and asked "Can't you read?" I looked at him and said "Of course I can. Why are you asking this?" He replied that there was a big sign on top of the entrance door, which said the Embassy was closed. I told him that I truly did not notice the sign. And then he replied "Why are you here? What do you want?" I said that I would like to go to Australia for a visit. He gave me an application form and asked me to fill it in and leave my passport with him; then he would see what he could do. He asked me what was my occupation and I explained to him about my clinic and my job. A week after my passport was delivered to my door with two months visa. At the time the law by Australian Embassy was to have a return ticket and $10,000 spending money to get a visa, which I did not have. I strongly believe that was ***another miracle of God*** as he promised me.

When I got the visa, my husband, as usual, accused me of doing something inappropriate to get it. I paid no attention, as I knew it was God's miracle and I never mentioned that to anybody. I was happy and I believed that I was going to be saved from my horrible situation. I was very sick. I looked like an anorexic and wherever I went they tested me for drug abuse but it was due to lots of prescribed medication, antidepressants, painkillers and sleeping tablets. Because of all these I was always dopey and I could hardly eat and many time

I had to have a drip. Because of that, everyone talked to my husband to let me go. That was how he gave me his permission to come for a month holiday. However, he did not want me to take my little girl who was at that time six years old; as he was worried that I would not come back. Therefore, he took her over to his parents' house. Three days after he called me to go to hospital as my daughter was almost dying. Apparently, the whole three days she refused to eat and was crying for me, since I didn't have any contact with her during that time. Then, she started to have vomiting and have bad stomach pains. The doctor in hospital said to her father that there was nothing wrong with our daughter physically but she is very stressed and emotional and if she didn't see me she could die. That was when my husband decided to inform me and asked me to go to the hospital to see my daughter. As soon as she saw me, she ran into my arms and became well and happy straight away. My husband was angry when he saw how she reacted to me and told me that she was the same as me. That was why he gave his permission to take my daughter with me on my holiday.

## Chapter 2

# My life in Australia

I LEFT IRAN IN 1987 and flew to Australia with my daughter. I made an arrangement for my 2 sons who were 16 and 15 at the time, to escape Iran illegally as they were both due for military service. It was a very risky business and I had to pay a big money to the people who organised these escapes. You pay big money while you do not know if they will arrive safely! A week before this a mini bus full of people got shot during the border crossing. I discussed everything with my two sons and they agreed to that arrangement. I arrived in Sydney; my aunt and her husband came to pick me up and I went to their house. They were living with their two daughters at the time. Their oldest daughter was married and had three children and they used to come and visit her parents on weekends. They had a small house and there was no spare room for my daughter and me. My daughter and I were sleeping on a foam single mattress on the floor. It was very hard for me and also for my aunt's family. I was very allergic to cigarette smoke and they were both smoking in the house, so on two occasions I had to be taken to hospital because of respiratory problems. I could not say anything, as I was a guest in their home. I had some money so I offered my aunt to buy a caravan and live in their backyard; but she refused and said if I was not happy, I should leave. They did not support me and I was terrified to be alone with my daughter in a new country.

The second day after my arrival I went to immigration office and applied for humanitarian visa. I gave them all the information relating to my life in Iran. I tried to enrol my daughter at a school but they would not accept her until I had a residency. They gave me a temporary work permit to support my daughter and myself. I used to pray on my pray mat and cry for my two sons to arrive safely. One day after, my aunt asked me to leave. I started walking with my little girl while crying and praying to God to help me. As I was walking, I saw a statue of Mary, which I felt was looking at me, smiling and guiding me to the building that I did not know what it was. I went with my daughter to the building; my face was soaked with tears. As I went inside the building, a lady came toward me with a smile and asked what was wrong. I was too upset even to reply. She took my daughter and me to her office and introduced herself. She said, "I am a nun and I'm the principal of this catholic private school". I started to explain my situation to her. I said that I have to leave my aunt's house and that I was scared to be by myself. I had some money but that money was mostly for my two sons' expenses to be able to join me later on. The sister was very kind and immediately said that my daughter could start her education in that school from the day after and that I could work there as a teacher's assistant in kindergarten. She said they would find me a safe accommodation, as well. She came with me to my auntie's house and we informed her about the situation. I only stayed one more month in their house. Altogether I was at their house for around two months. I strongly believe that the nun's help was *another miracle of God*.

I used to work at the school for only two hours a day; therefore I had plenty of time to look for a job in my field. I found a job in a small beauty salon. As they were not recognising my qualifications the only job they would give me was body massage that I have never done in my life. The employer only showed me how to do it. I went to the government department for recognition of my qualification. The first option was to go and study which was impossible under the circumstances. The second option was to sit for a test that was sat out by government for a beauty therapist and also hair dressing. I sat for both tests and passed them. I was qualified to be a beauty therapist and hairdresser by the Australian Government, then. They also recognised my Cosmetologist Degree from France.

I came to Australia but it didn't stop my husband insulting me as he would call at least twice a day and offense me by his verbal vicious. That made me to file for divorce from Australia. I got divorce but I kept in touch just for my daughter as I believe children should not be disconnecting with their parents.

I found a job in a beauty and weight loss centre for $9.00 per hour and I was working from 9 am until 6 pm. The nun found me a room next to a church and there was also a school next to the church. Therefore my daughter enrolled in that school and I started my new job. I would take my daughter to school at 8.30 and then I had to teach my little girl to come home in the afternoon, go to our room, close the door and watch TV until I came home. I bought a safety lock with alarm and told her to lock it as soon as she got in and not to open the door until I came home. I also took her with me to work on Saturdays and she would play or read until I finished work. The room next to the church was safe but was not quiet as the church had always–different functions. We had to share the same bathroom as the churchgoers. The first furniture we had was given to us from the church. I got a very bad eye infection that caused me temporary blindness and the minister's wife was looking after my daughter and me for a couple of days. The minister and his wife were very kind to us and they gave us lot of support, *another miracle of God.*

I progressed in my job very well and the salon became very busy. The owner left the whole business to be run by me as she was living in Sydney. There was no other employee there except me. The owner used to come only on Fridays to do the banking. I was making around $2,500 a week for her. She was very pleased and promised me a partnership in the business. My wages were $500 a week and she used to deduct $150 for tax. After about 6 months, she decided to sell the business without notifying me. One day she brought a young girl who was a hairdresser and told me that she was going to help me out in the salon. She asked me to train her. I was very happy to do so as I was doing so much by myself. I trained the girl in every aspect of the business. A week after one day the owner came down and told me that the girl was the new owner and from then on I would be working for her. I almost passed out and told her that she deceived me. She replied "You will learn. That's business". I said that I would not work for the young girl and would leave. The young girl said that she bought the business because I was running it and the owner promised her that I would stay. I was badly hurt and left. While I was working for her, because of working so hard, I was bleeding all the time. By then I'd saved some money and rented a two-bedroom house in the city. I bought some basic equipment, made one of the bedrooms as my working room and started working from home. I advertised in the newspaper with my picture and that was enough for all the clients from the previous salon to follow me. Unfortunately, the poor young girl lost the business. At the end of financial year, I went to claim my tax back and they told me that there was only two weeks pay. I did not know anything about the taxation system and since I was paid in cash, there was no proof of my income. Therefore I lost a lot of my hard earned money. I rang her and asked how she could have treated me that way. What she did to me was not fair. I told her if she believed in God, that God was watching her.

On one cloudy day I decided to go swimming with my daughter. At the end of the day, when I came back home, my skin was burned all over and swollen with fever and pain. I had to call radio doctor and she had to puncture all the blisters and gave me ointment to put over my skin. It took over a week to heal and I learnt my lesson. I have never ever gone out swimming in the middle of the day, even on a cloudy day, as I realised that the sun is much stronger in

Australia than anywhere else. Another day I went with my daughter sightseeing on a hot sunny day on a train. When I came back at the end of the day, I felt dizzy and nauseous and fainted at the train station. They took me to the hospital. I was informed I had sunstroke and that I should be wearing a hat when I go outside for any length of time.

I was bleeding heavily for months and doctor kept putting me on different medication to control the bleeding. They asked me to take it easy and rest which was impossible as I had to earn my living. The bleeding got worse and the gynaecologist had to arrange for immediate hysterectomy as the condition was life threatening. I was worried about my little girl, as I had nobody here to look after her. I had a client who was very nice and kind to us. She was living by herself and told me on many occasions that if I ever needed help, she would be there for me. So I asked her if she could look after my daughter while I was in hospital. She agreed immediately and came in the morning, took me to hospital and took my daughter to her house. Every afternoon she was my only visitor. I've never forgotten her kindness until this day. She is my spiritual sister and my children call her "auntie". The operation was successful but after three days, I started to have fever (it fluctuated between 40°C to 42°C). I was very nauseous and very sore as in those days the cut was very long. I was sure I had developed an infection. But every time I told the doctor or nurses about that, they looked at me and said that the problem was only in my mind as I had no one here and I was homesick. This continued for 17 days. My GP, who was informed by the hospital about my situation, contacted my auntie and asked her to come and visit me. She came to the hospital and maliciously said "I prayed to God to make you suffer but not to kill you!" My friend arrived with my daughter at the same time and my auntie insisted on taking my daughter that night to her house. I was told by my daughter later that she terrified my daughter by telling her "Don't worry, it is obvious your mum is going to die. If she dies, I will look after you".

On the 17th day I told my friend who was looking after my daughter that "I don't think I can take it anymore. If you come tomorrow and find me dead, send my daughter back to my family in Iran, please". I could hardly talk and was so weak that I could not even walk to the bathroom by myself. Every time I asked the nurses to help me, they said "You can walk". I was shivering and had fever, so I asked if they could help me to drink a glass of water. Their response was "You have two hands". An Australian patient, in the next bed, felt very bad for me as they were treating her totally different comparing with me. She used to help me to go to the bathroom or drink some water and was apologising to me for the hospital staff cruel behaviour towards me. Every time the surgeon or the hospital doctor came to see me I kept telling them that I have infection and my stomach was the size of a 5 month old pregnancy and I needed antibiotic but they still insisted that I was just homesick and alone and depressed. During that night, I prayed to God to save me or take me.

I started reading the 20 versus of Koran that I read every night before going to sleep. I was repeating them over and over. All of a sudden at midnight the infection in my body poured out from my tummy area through the pores in my skin. I was covered in pus; I called the nurse. When she came she was shocked and immediately called the doctor. The doctor thought that my stiches burst. The nurse cleaned me up and the doctor saw with his own eyes that the infection was coming out through the pores in my skin and not the stiches. Finally they believed that I had infection and they put me on strong antibiotics. My fever dropped down immediately and I had the best sleep. The next morning I woke up, had a shower by myself and felt alive again, ***another miracle of God***.

In the morning, the doctor came and apologised for ignoring my condition and put it down to homesickness. He was fascinated by what happened that night before and was questioning me how it happened and what I did? I told him that I prayed and that this is a miracle of God. I asked him to release me, as I wanted to go home. He responded, "You have a very bad infection and you can't go home". I laughed and said "You and all the staff in this hospital ignored me with my serious life threatening condition for the last two weeks and now you are concerned? I am not staying in this hospital even one more day and I release myself." They released me and I went home, but the hospital doctor and a nurse used to come and visit me at home every day for one week. I continuously had infection in my ovaries and therefore had to take antibiotic and painkillers for two years. If I stopped taking the medication the infection would return. Every time I questioned the gynaecologist he would give me different medication but I knew there was something wrong with my ovaries. One day one of my client who was aware of my situation, offered me to take me to her gynaecologist who was in Sydney and get a second opinion. She took me there. He knew the gynaecologist who did my original operation. After checking me up, he said that I needed an immediate operation on both of my ovaries. So he told me to go back to my gynaecologist and he would inform him of my condition to arrange the operation. I went back to see him, had my operation and received yet another apology from him. Within six weeks, I recovered and all the pain was gone and I did not have to use any more painkillers or antibiotics. My gynaecologist caused all the suffering and pain that I went through.

I was informed that my two boys were kept in the prison on the Pakistan border by my family in Iran. They were asking for more money to release them. I asked my mother to go and get them and look after them until they came to Australia. I accepted to pay for everything. So, she flew to the Pakistan, paid for their release, went to the capital city and got a room in a hotel. From then on we could keep in touch. Get them up to this stage was ***another miracle of God***. One day I was watching the news in Australia and I heard on the news the hotel that my mother and my sons were staying was bombed and totally gone. I had a cardiac attack and was taken to the hospital by ambulance. After one day, I came back home and tried to contact my relatives in Iran to find some information. Two days later my mother called; that was the happiest moment in my life. She said just two hours before the bombing they left the hotel to town to do some shopping. But all their belongings were gone. I immediately sent them some money to go to another hotel. They went to Australian Embassy and applied for residency. I was also under the procedure of my residency in Australia. I was praying and crying every night on my prayer mat to bring my two sons to me in Australia. One night, during praying, a vision came to me that my two sons knocked on the front door; I opened the door and held them in my arms. It was so real but I still took it for a dream. It was the day before my birthday the doorbell rang and my two sons were at the front door. I was speechless and I just held them in my arms and was screaming, laughing and thanking God, all at the same time; **another miracle of God**. They said they got their residency and my mother bought them the tickets, put them on the plane. She told them when they got to Australia to get a taxi and go to my house. They also told me that they had a lot of hard time while passing through the border and jail but they were lucky that they were not abused. But they were scarred. They had to spend most of their time in a room at hotel because they had no identification. My oldest son got malaria and nearly died. One day when they were going to Australian Embassy they were on a bus and the bus was full of people. Just two stops before the Embassy they decided to get off the bus and walk to the Embassy. In next stop, a suicide bomber blew up the bus and no one was survived, **another miracle of God**. Therefore, the boys had lots of emotional problems.

When my sons arrived I thought that finally we were going to have a peaceful life together. I also was a legal guardian for 2 Australian citizen boys, same age as my sons, for about 2 years as they were living with an abusive father in my neighbourhood. I used to give them food and help them with their schoolwork. The father used to bash them up; one day, when he was bashing them up badly, they ran to my house. He still followed them there and hitting them in front of me and my little girl. I had to call the police for help. When the police arrived the 2 boys were holding on to my legs and begging me to let them stay with me. The police said that if I agreed we could go to the court, I could become their legal guardian and we got a domestic violence order against the father. That was how I became their legal guardian. I started taking care of them, helped with their study and working on their social skills and I managed to make two gentlemen from these boys that had criminal record like shoplifting, fighting, etc. Sometimes they got expelled from school and the principal put them on probation. Within a year, the principal sent me a letter and congratulated me for bringing up the boys so well. I had to look after five children plus working, studying and still suffering from ill health. After six months looking after these two boys, I went to seek advice from the Chamber Magistrate regarding getting some subsidy for those boys. I found out that they were already receiving government payment that we were not aware of; but the cheques were being sent to their father. The Chamber Magistrate arranged to have the cheques sent to me from then on.

One of my clients gave me free family ticket to the Australian Wonderland. We were picked up and returned by a bus for the whole day. While we were in Wonderland my handbag was stolen that had my passports, some money and my credit cards and also the children's belongings, like a watch, necklace etc. By the time I informed the bank about my credit cards they'd already spent $2,000 on my two credit cards. The bank told me that I was responsible for this debt but anything after that the bank would cover it. So our happy day turned to a lot of heartache. I lost my grocery money plus all my documents. Everything was reported to the police and Wonderland security but nothing was found until this day.

While I was working for myself from the room in the house, a business lady, who was involved with a cosmetic company, approached me, as she was very impressed with my knowledge and my work. She offered me to go into a beauty business with her; she would put up the money and I would run the business for her. I accepted, as it was a good offer. She had a big Victorian house in the middle of town with six bedrooms and a huge living area. They converted the three front bedrooms into a beauty salon and I was living at the back with the five children. I started working for her from 9 am until 6 pm six days a week for $150 per week plus rent free accommodation. She promised me a 50/50 partnership in the business. I was very happy with her offer and trusted her with all my heart. She used to come down with her family on weekends and I catered for them as well as my family. I was very happy for a short time until one day she did not come down on weekend to pay me my money. Therefore I went to the bank to get my money. The bank manager informed me that I couldn't take any money out. I got very upset and told him that I was the one who was banking the money there every day and that I was a partner in the business. He informed me that I am not a partner. The lady and her husband were the partners. It hurt me extremely as I realised that another person took advantage of me because I was not aware of rules and regulations. I went to the Chamber Magistrate and showed him the contract that I had. He informed me that by that contract I was obligated to work for her as long as I lived and everything I had, including my personal belongings, was hers. I was only earning 50% of the salon's income after all the expenses were paid, i.e. the phone bill, water, electricity, gas, rates; any repairs that were required on the building and all business expenses, i.e. equipments, etc. Because of all that I was only getting $150 a week from $2,000 to $2,500 weekly income. She did not even give me a chance to recover after my operation and within 3 days after arriving home from the hospital she fully booked me for work. Even my clients were feeling sorry for me because I had to work on them while I was not well.

Few months later, after all the battle with emigration department I received a shocking letter informing me that I had to leave Australia with my daughter within a week. I was devastated. I had a client that morning who was a media reporter. When she saw me crying and found out about the letter, she said that it did not make any sense. How could they give residency to my two sons and deport my daughter and me? Within an hour, I had all the media in my house. I was interviewed by a current affair program and the program was aired on TV that night. Because of the interest my case generated, my story was on the air for almost six months as other people who were interested in my case were interviewed. All the newspapers also covered my case as well. As a result of all those pressure, I ended up in the intensive care unit couple of times. One night, when I was praying and crying I heard strong voice telling me "Do not worry, my child. I will send my army to help you and get you out of this situation." I was reading about my case in the local newspaper every day and watching the program on TV every night, while I'd only agreed to one interview. People from all over Australia were supporting me. I was receiving thousands of letters through the local newspaper and different communities that sent their representatives to Canberra to plead my case. Churches made strong petitions on my behalf and the head of one of the churches announced that the church would support me and my children; and they would not allow us to be deported because they were aware of what would happen to me if I returned to Iran because of the political situation. Even though I practised Islam I did not agree with the Islamic rule of being covered from head to toe and not wearing makeup or nail polish. I came to Australia seeking a different life such as women rights, equality and freedom. Lots of politicians without knowing or seeing me sent documentation to the immigration department to support my case regarding the danger I would face if I were to return to Iran.

I had a phone call from ASIO regarding my case asking me to stop my communication with all the media as I had caused enough response in the media. I obeyed their instruction and I did not accept any more phone calls or interviews. Following that I had a phone call from an agent telling me that if I wanted to stay in Australia he was willing to help me as long as I follow his instructions. He was from another state and asked my little girl and me, since we were the deportees, to go there; and he and his family would come and pick us up from the airport. He arranged for the plane tickets and my sons could join us later on. But I had to go first to make all the necessary arrangements. As I was desperate and had no choice, I went with my daughter but I gave all the information to the pastor who was helping and supporting me. When I arrived there the agent came, and took me to a government building. I had to sign hundreds of pages to make sure I am truly here with my children for a peaceful life. And that I would not be politically active. I was amazed how much information they had about me and my whole family. I made an agreement to move from NSW to Victoria. They arranged accommodation and helped me with removal of my belongings. Therefore we moved to a place where we didn't know anybody or anything.

As soon as we arrived, I received a letter informing me that my deportation was waived and my application for residency was in progress. The boys and my daughter were very unhappy in that new place. They just made some friends in our previous home and they had to start adjusting again to another environment. I also lost all my clients but the contract that I had with my previous employer was not valid anymore because I was not a resident of Australia. Therefore I had my freedom in the workplace at least. I learnt a valuable lesson; not to go into business with anybody as I had two bad experiences. The two foster boys were removed from my care because I was not an Australian resident. That devastated all of us but we had to obey. I was so sick and on lots of medications; taking 14 sleeping tablets a day to be able to cope and get at least some sleep. Several times I ended up in intensive care and I was under the care of a psychiatrist and a psychologist. After two months the government stopped supporting me and I went to social security and they arranged student allowance for the boys but not for my daughter and me. The allowance would not even cover our rent. I got some help from numerous charities and also a lovely Australian elderly couple who would do grocery shopping for us on a weekly basis. They were of the people who heard about my case from the current affair program. I tried to find a job but I was not successful. I tried to work from home but that did not succeed either. We were all getting more and more depressed and my younger son and I developed an allergic asthma as well. I also had to walk long distances to do shopping and to the children's school as we were in an isolated area far from any facilities. My father managed to send me some money to buy a second hand car, so I bought a station wagon in the hope that I might be able to find some work by going to people's homes.

After five months living in Victoria, I decided to move back to NSW as I could not continue living the way we were. I started ringing different removalists but as soon as I mentioned my name, they refused to move me. They were still observing all my activities. Apparently, I was not allowed to go back and all my phone calls were monitored. Most of my clients were still in contact with me and were asking me to come back. I drove back to where we used to live, found a two bedroom old house and paid its bond. I contacted the pastor and his wife and he hired a truck under his name. We put my car in the truck and drove back together by the truck. I contacted my children to start packing up our belongings. After only a couple of hours sleep we packed up the truck and headed back to NSW. I drove my car back and the pastor drove the truck. The agent in charge of my case came and gave me a dirty look but could not say anything as the pastor was there helping us. The pastor was aware of my situation. We moved back to "our" town! We were all happy to be back.

The pastor helped me to convert a little garage under the house into a room so that I could start working as I had my clients waiting for me. I decorated the whole wall by cutting pictures from magazines and bought some second hand equipment and furniture. The house was situated in a very noisy street and close to a busy hotel, which was causing lots of disturbance. One night I could hear two men trying to rape a girl under my window. I was so upset and scared. I went to the back room and called the police and gave them all the required information, hoping that they would come and help the girl. The police came within a couple of minutes. As soon as the men heard the police they covered the girl's mouth so that she could not scream. They were hiding behind a big tree. The police got out of the car, looked around and got back in the car and left. I was traumatised by such an incident, as I could do nothing. After a while the men left and the girl also left. I did not dare to come out of the house.

One morning after dropping my children at school, I came back home, went to the laundry to do some washing. As I got to the laundry, which was next to the garage under the house, a young drunk man who was already there, grabbed me and pushed me against the wall before I got a chance to do anything. As I hit my head, I went limp; he raped me and then left. I was devastated and shocked. I went to my doctor and asked him to check me up in case of any sexually transmitted diseases. He told me that I should report it to the police. I replied that I couldn't do that. First of all I did not know who the man was; secondly, that would hurt my children. I just prayed to God that I will not any lasting effect from that experience. It took me years to recover from that incident and I was having regular checkups to make sure that I did not catch any disease. I was not accepting any male clients as a single woman I could not trust them as I had an unpleasant experience with one of my client's husband.

Unfortunately, in every society, when you are a single woman, majority of men think that you are available and do not respect you the way they respect a married woman. I never felt comfortable in the company of a married couple. I still did not have my residency and I could even hardly manage my rent. I was looking for a new family doctor as I could not even afford to pay my doctor's fee as my family doctor, who was an Iranian lady, would never see me before charging me and had no compassion for anybody. She did not help me in any way during the two years that I was her patient. One of my clients referred me to her family doctor who was very kind and understanding. He would not charge me and often gave me free medicine sample, too. He was aware of my situation and had been following my story through the local newspaper. My case was followed up in the local newspaper for over a year until I received my residency.

When we came back to NSW I received a letter from immigration department regarding a medical examination for my daughter and myself. The medical examiner said that my daughter, who was 10 at the time, had a birth defect in her eyes and would become blind. Therefore we could not proceed with the residency. This news was devastating to all of us. I went back to our family doctor and he sent us to a very good eye specialist. During the weeks of waiting to see the eye specialist, my children and I were very sad and worried for my daughter. When the specialist examined my daughter, he immediately responded, "Your daughter just needs some glasses and the medical examiner's diagnosis is a total nonsense", **another miracle of God**. He wrote a strong letter stating his diagnosis and he sent the letter to the medical examiner to change his report. Therefore, everything went ahead and we got our residency.

While I was struggling to cope with my personal life and health, I never stopped helping in need people. I was doing interpreting for some Iranian refugees on a voluntary basis and helping them with any other issues as requested. There was an Iranian family (two sisters, one brother and their families) who had problem with their residential status and also some legal matters. I supported them and did all the interpreting work free of charge. One of the ladies, whom I helped to win her case about substantial amount of money in the court, promised me that if she won her case she would share the money with me, as a gratitude for my help all through the year for all her family. The two sisters came to my door when the case was finished. I opened the door and welcomed them as usual. They pushed me in and abused me verbally in front of my children. That shocked me; I started to tremble and I fainted. One of the neighbours called police when they heard the yelling and screaming. By the time police arrived they had left and police had to take me to hospital. The police charged the two sisters for domestic violence. I was so hurt, it was Ramadan and I was fasting. I used to pray and cry and talk to God how these people could do this to me while I did everything in my power to help them and not to ask for anything in return. I still cannot understand how those people could abuse me in such a way as I did nothing wrong to them. We went through the courts and all the punishment they got for almost killing me was an apprehended violence order. All of the Iranian community in my area were very upset by that incident. After a few months, I had a phone call from a Justice of Peace asking me to go and see those two sisters; as they realised what they did to me was wrong and wanted to apologise. I could not face them anymore. The husband and their brother personally apologised to me for their behaviour. That incident affected my children very badly, especially my two teenage boys. After about one year, an Iranian lady came to me and said accept their apology, please as they deeply regret what they have done to you. One of the sisters, who had two sons was more upset as her two sons were not well; one had a hole in his heart and the other had a brain tumour. She felt that she was going through this pain and suffering for what she'd done to me and my children. I responded that I have forgiven them and I was sorry to hear about her children. I would pray for the two sons to recover. In fact, I could never wish anything bad for anyone, even the one who has hurt me. I believe they need more pray than anyone else. Afterwards, I heard that her two sons fully recovered and they are in good health. However, her husband left her as he was very disappointed with his wife's behaviour in general and the other sister married for the second time and divorced under very bad circumstances and suffered with a very bad karma. To this day, whenever they see me anywhere they stay far away from me and obey their AVO.

The Muslims' fasting lasts for 30 days and means nothing to eat or drink from sunrise to sunset. At the end of the month, the grocery money that would normally be spent for the whole family should be given to a poor family. The philosophy is to have a benefit of a detoxification to your body and understanding the hunger feeling of the poor. I did not do the fasting in the right way as I did not eat anything before sunrise and never ate immediately after sunset so my fasting actually lasted for 24 hours. During one Ramadan, I was fasting. I used to get up before sun rise, do my prayer, have a glass of water and my medication and start my fasting and then ended it after sun set (sometimes even two hours after sun set) with some light meal. All day I was working and doing my household duties. On the 21st day of the Ramadan at night I started to have very bad stomach pain and indigestion (non-stop burping). I called the radio doctor and he diagnosed me with hiatus hernia He said if I continued fasting, it could kill me. Therefore, that was my last day of fasting in my life. Even to this day, I cannot go without food for more than a few hours.

Because I was on so many medications I did not have any appetite and I was malnourished and underweight which was almost at the stage of being anorexic. My doctor did a whole check up as I was losing weight rapidly but did not find any life threatening diseases and continued with the same medications as previously—**I had to take two kinds of antibiotics continuously to control the infection in my body, painkillers and anti-inflammatory medication to cope with the constant pain, heart tablets, antidepressants, sleeping tablets, antihistamine and cortisone in the form of tablets, cream and injections.** As I was taking so many medications I started to have problems with my kidneys. My GP sent me to kidney specialist. After all the routine tests he advised me that I need to have a surgery as I had a lot of kidney stones. I was in crucial pain, which on many occasion the radio doctor had to give me morphine injections. I believe kidney pain is worst than childbirth. I was supposed to have the operation within a month as I had to wait for a public hospital. One of my clients, who was a naturopath, gave me some natural remedies which resulted in lots of pain and agony; but I felt a lot more better after a couple of days and my kidney pain was totally gone. I went to the specialist and said I wanted to have another scan before going to the operation as I had no kidney pain. They arranged for the scan to be done in the early morning before operation. When I've got there, I informed the doctor that I was allergic to iodine but the doctor said "This is a different dye that we are using and you will be fine". They put the first lot and did some scan. As he started to do the second one I felt burning sensation all over my body and asked the doctor to stop. But I passed out before I could say another word. After three days I opened my eyes in the intensive care unit. I tried to speak but I couldn't. The hospital rang my children's school to advise them what happened to me and my poor children were terrified coming to hospital and looking at me in that situation. It took over a week until I could function normally again. The doctor in charge was apologising for not listening to me and making sure I would not sue him. The result of the scan was that my kidneys were totally free of any stones and I did not need to go for the operation. I believe that was **another miracle of God**.

I started to have allergic reaction to a lot of my medications. The only thing I could still take was Mogadon, my sleeping tablet. I continued to take more natural remedies and went through lots of healing crisis, which is the procedure of the body to eliminate the toxins and heal itself. I started to investigate and study about natural therapy and that was how I began to look into the field. While I was sick and struggling with all the other issues in my life I started to study different modality in natural therapy. I qualified in aromatherapy, polarity therapy, kinesiology, naturopathy, homeopathy, acupuncture and etc. by correspondence method through different institutions and finally in science degree majoring in nutrition at the age of 50. The more knowledge I achieved the more I could help myself and others in a totally different aspect to my previous belief.

As I started to use all these natural remedies I had horrible headaches, feeling like an explosion was happening in my head. I was losing my balance. It was also affecting my eyesight and made a lot of weight lost to me. My GP sent me to an endocrinologist for my condition. After examinations, he said I had a brain tumour in front of my children. I had to go to Prince Henry Hospital for further tests, which would take all day. It brought more misery and pain to my children and me. Within a week I went to the hospital. They did all the necessary tests on me and I was released at the end of the day. After another week I went to see the specialist for my results and in meanwhile my children and I were praying. When I saw the specialist he was quiet and very surprised, as he had to announce to me that there is no tumour, ***another miracle of God***. He could not understand why I had all those symptoms. He did not even apologise to put my children and me through the hell because of his misdiagnosis.

One day, while I was going through the healing crisis, a friend offered to take me to a Buddhist Temple in Bundanoon as an important monk was coming. People from all around the world were coming to see him. It was my first time to go to a Buddhist Temple. I was very sick, so they had to put me in the back of a van, lying down, as I could not sit up. The Temple was very new and the building construction was not completed yet; that was the reason for the important monk to come. My friend converted to Buddhism and was very devoted. It was a huge gathering and all the monks were sitting up on a stage and the nuns, dressed in pure white, were sitting in the first row. The important monk started lecturing that was followed by meditation. When the meditation finished, the important monk pointed to the area where I was leaning against a wall. Everyone looked to see whom he is pointing at and the next thing, one of the nuns came toward me and asked me to go with her. She had to help me to walk toward the stage. She guided me to sit in front of all the nuns and then the monk told me "Just look at me". I kept looking at him and I was feeling sleepy. After a while, he finished the ceremony. I had no idea what was happening but I felt a big relief. I could stand on my feet. I asked the nun why he chose me. The nun replied "For us to become nun or monk, we have to go through lots of suffering and pain. The important monk who can feel and see things could feel that you have gone through enough suffering and pain to be eligible to come and sit in front of all of us." The reason for him looking into my eyes was that is how a monk performs healing. He took away some of my pain, especially the pain in my heart which was a burning pain. In the afternoon the main monk could not come and perform the meditation ceremony and another monk performed it. I asked the monk where the important monk was. He informed me that he was sick in bed with the pain that he took from my heart. He was resting in his "Kuti" to heal himself and would talk to me the day after (Kuti is a small one-room house that the monks live in). The next day I went to see the monk. I sat in front of his Kuti and told him thanked him for taking all that pain from my heart after many years. He replied "You have suffered more than what anyone could suffer through several life times. You are blessed and you are going to be a healer and help many other sick and suffering human beings as you have done all your life anyway". He gave me his book and a small ornament. He asked me to put it in my business area to help me with the financial crisis I was experiencing. I asked him "What have I done to deserve all this suffering and when is it going to end?" He said "Even though you have done nothing wrong in your life but this is your Karma from your past lives as this is your fulfilment life. You are going to be helping and healing others and your life will get better as you get older." At the time, as I was sick and dying, I had no idea about what he said. But on the way back I felt a bit better as I could sit up on the journey back.

When I got back, my friend offered to take me to a music class. I knew how to play piano but I had not touched a piano for years. I thought that would be nice to get in touch with music again. The first day I went to the class the teacher looked at me intensely which made me uncomfortable but he tried to mask it. After about three sessions, at the end of the class he asked me if I wanted to go for a coffee and a chat. We ended up as close friends and he was also teaching music to my daughter. He was a very nice Australian man, who was never married before. He fell madly in love with me; from the first moment he saw me, he said, it was like he had known me for years. For me, having someone who cared about me during all my sicknesses and other personal battles was very comforting. I also helped him emotionally as he had lots of childhood scares and lost his mother recently due to a cancer. My children could not accept this relationship. After four years, even though he wanted to marry me, I had to let him go since he could not share my love and caring with my children.

My two sons finished their high school certificate in a selective high school and both got into university. Because of that, I decided to move closer to the university. My oldest son got a weekend job working in a café while he was studying at University for $5.00 per hour. One day the owner asked him to clean the glass door in the café. While he was cleaning it, he fell and the broken glass cut his forearm very deeply. He lost a lot of blood and was taken to hospital for stiches. The owner brought him home and I received another shock when I saw my son. At this stage we were not able to financially cope. I had to provide him with lots of good nutrition to replace all the blood that he lost but the owner did not compensate my son for that accident even though it happened during working hours. He did not even call to see how my son was going. He was also our landlord who used to come every fortnight to collect his rent. The house was in a very bad condition and he would not pay any attention to the repairs of the house, as well. I looked after my son and after a while, he was better and able to return to his weekend job.

Since I decided to look for another accommodation closer to the University, I gave a verbal notice to our landlord that we would be moving in a couple of weeks. After we moved, he took us to the court and accused me of not giving him any notice. I was ordered to pay him three weeks rent. My son had to work for many weekends for free to pay this debt off. I could financially manage only with the help of different charity organisations. At one stage that I could not get any help from any of these organisations, I was praying to God for help. One day, a postman knocked on the door and gave me an envelope with a cheque for $500; until this day, I do not know where the money came from, ***another miracle of God***.

My daughter used to sleep with me. When I cried and prayed at nights, she would say something unusual for her age. I asked her "Who told you these things?" "Angels told me to tell you", she replied. Many times her phrases would calm me down and I could go to sleep. At the time, I thought nothing about Angels except in the concept of children's books. I also remembered that before she was born I had a dream about Mary and Fatima who told me she is going to be a special girl. She was very wise, calm and kind; she went through a lot of hardship, especially at school as she struggled with a new language and culture as well as watching all the problems her mother went through. One night she told me "Mum I've been praying and asking the Angels to give me a room with pink furniture for myself". I replied "One day you will have it". I was looking for our new place near the university to rent. I went to see a house, which was an old and broken fibro house. There was a little room with all brand new build-in pink furniture. The room did not seem to be part of the house and made me to cry, remembering my daughter's wish. I asked the landlord how this was possible; because the rest of the house was old. He explained the previous owner was a carpenter. He built this room for his granddaughter who used to come interstate and stay with him during holidays. I rented the house; I thought that was **another miracle of God** for my daughter. She was over the moon and so happy! There was a garage at the side of the house which I converted it to a clinic with the help of my children and a friend. I put a little sign at the front, too. I continued my work as an interpreter which by then, after finishing interpreting and translating degree, I was getting paid for the service, as well.

Even though I was constantly suffering from aches and sicknesses, I learned to live with it; I continued to be both mother and father to my children, worked and studied natural therapy modalities by correspondence. Most of the time, I cooked our meals, did my housework and studied at night when the children were slept. I used to survive on 4 hours sleep a night and I could only manage that because I was doing yoga and meditation. My business started to improve. One day, a lady walked in and offered to transfer all their clients of a franchise weight loss business to me. I asked her why she chose me from all the other clinics in the city. She replied your educational background was more important to me than the location of your salon. Therefore, my business became very busy and I did specialised training with their company and I still work with them until now. To me this was ***another miracle of God***.

I was still doing interpreting jobs as I enjoyed helping people who came to this country but did not know the language or culture. Lots of clinics and hospitals would send complimentary letters to my coordinator stating how good I was at my job and commenting that I did a lot of voluntary work as well. One day my coordinator called me and said that she received lots of letters complimenting my work. I was expecting to be congratulated and thanked for my good work but instead she turned around and accused me of trying to take her job from her. She said that she would not sack me but I wouldn't receive any work from her. I was so disappointed with this treatment and decided to approach the Discrimination Board. We attended a reconciliation meeting and everything was worked out on the surface but I only received no more than one job a year from her since then. This incident hurt me for days especially as I realised that there is no justice even here in this "free" and democratic country. I still wanted to help people as they used to come to my door or call me for help but I was stopped. I was not allowed to do that is as it was a social worker job. People started a petition and asking for my services but it was ignored and I was replaced.

I was sad to lose a good and regular income from my interpreting but thanks God my business was blossoming and made up for that loss. On the night of my 40th birthday, I was very sick as I had two more operations in a short period of time on my upper jaw due to inflammation and infection. Even though I was taking natural remedies, I still had to deal with lots of healing crisis. I was praying on my pray mat and was crying and begging God to take me as I could not cope with any more pain or sickness. While I was praying, an Angel appeared to me. The Angel I envisioned gave me a big tub of a golden honey-like substance; she commenced to pour it all over my body and meanwhile enlightened me. From that point onwards, I could see and communicate with angels and the spirit of the deceased. I had never even believed in the possibility of such things. When this happened to me, even though I felt so warm and loved but I thought I was dying; that was why I could see Angels and spirits of my beloved deceased ones. I thought they came to take me. I opened my eyes and closed them, but it did not make any differences; I could still see them.

I could hardly sleep all that night; and I found myself still alive in the morning. I went to the kitchen and made myself a sandwich and ate it all! As prior to this incident I could hardly finish a sandwich through the whole day. My children looked at me and said "Mum, you look different. You are glowing and you are eating!" I did not say anything regarding the Angel's visit. I went to my GP and I asked him to send me for a scan of my brain. He asked "Why" and I replied, "I think have become mad". He said he could not see any sign of insanity. I replied, "When I tell you all details, you will accept that I am mad". I explained everything to him. He listened and asked me how I felt. I said my feeling was better than ever I could remember and I had a good breakfast. He replied "That's beautiful and you do not need any brain scan". An Angel touched me on my head on the night after but I was still terrified since I didn't know what exactly was happening to me. I started my search to understand what I am going through.

I went to the churches; spoke to priests, pastors, nuns and etc. as I was trying to understand what was happening to me. I contacted many spiritual people and started reading lots of spiritual books. I started to understand a bit about what was happening. On the other hand, those clients who used to come for a facial and were suffering from headaches as well, confessed as I was massaging their faces they felt the heat coming out of my hands and made them feel much better. It took their pain away and some felt tingling and warm sensations through their whole body. I realised that I honoured a healing gift by the Angel. It had healed me and was given to heal others. I still kept it as a secret and did not announce myself as a healer until I was about 43 years old. I was praying and asking God to show me the way to be close to him because I was not feeling right anymore to pray in a Muslim way. I received a clear message saying I can reach Him anywhere and anytime. I did not have to pray on a specific time or a specific place. He said that He can hear and see me at any place and any time. That was the end of my Islamic practice.

I believe in God and Angelic Kingdom and unconditional love for all human being. I still say lots of my prayers and Koran verses as I have known them all my life. I have Koran above my house and clinic entrances. I believe I am born Muslim, I will die a Muslim but I have been chosen by God to practise the way I've done since age 40. I was questioning God to show me about reincarnation, as it is not believed in many religions. Thereafter I had so many real incidents in my life to be shown the past lives so clearly with some evidences. The answer was "Yes, reincarnation exists as the soul never dies. In different religions they believe in different forms. You have lived many lives and as this life is your fulfilment life you have come across people from your past life to rectify unresolved issues from the past." Whenever I met some body all throughout my life I would have a dream of those people in different time. I thought nothing of it and took it as a dream by then but after that conversation, I realised that I knew these people in my past lives.

I met three men within a couple of months apart in different places in one year. Every one of them wanted to marry me within 24 hours. They were not aware of the past life issues but I could clearly see myself with them in other life times. In one case, I asked God to show me a sign to know if it was real and not a dream.

I met an English man; I saw an Indian Prince every time I looked at him. He quickly wanted to marry me but it was not possible. I had no feelings for him and there was no compatibility. But it was a sense of knowing each other and being comfortable in each other's company. One day I asked him if he knew anything about India. He replied when he was a young boy, he used to sing in Indian and say some Indian words but his mother would tell him off. He also said that every time he looked at me, he saw an Indian Princess in me. I told him what I saw about him, as well. When I slept in my house, I had a strong vision of us in a big Indian castle. We were getting married in an Indian ceremony and as the Indian wedding custom; he put some red dye in the middle of my eyebrows. I felt it strongly that it made me to wake up. When I woke up, I looked at the mirror and saw an indentation in the middle of my eyebrows which I've never ever had it before. That was my proof from God to belief in reincarnation. About 16 years later I came across a book by Stuart Wilde, "The Art of Redemption". The book was opened on the page 203 with the heading "The Mark on the Forehead". It explained that people with the mark guides humans to safety. That explanation gave me another concept on top of my belief in reincarnation.

I explained to him about the past lives issues between us and he also agreed as he had so many strong and real visions and dreams about us which could not be at the present time. Many of those dreams and visions were happening to us simultaneously. We both agreed that there were no compatibilities between us at this time and we parted as friends.

One night I was having dinner with my friends. A French man came to our table, staring at me and started talking to me. I had no interest even talking to him but I could see him in a vision in a past life in France; we died in a war while we were holding hands. This man also wanted to marry me in a short time. He was going crazy with such a strong feeling in such a short time. I was aware of the past issues but he did not know anything about reincarnation. So for a couple of months I had hard time trying to persuade him that I had no feelings for him. He was also 11 years younger than me. We finally parted but not on good terms. About one month after the French guy, I met another man. Again I was having dinner with my friends and we ordered some drinks. As we wanted to pay, the waiter said that he already paid for the drinks. It was the same story as with the previous two men. He even came around to my house and introduced himself to my children. He was very nice and I felt some attraction to him, however, I also felt lots of fear and doubt toward him. I prayed to God and Angels to show me about him. I saw a strong vision from my past life that we were husband and wife and he was about to kill me but I managed to run away from the house. Then I realised why I could not trust him. I found out lots of bad things about him later on. He was a womaniser. I nicely told him to leave me alone as I could never trust him. I believe this was the way God proved to me about reincarnation.

I was tired of moving from one house to another. I'd changed 11 houses from 1987 to 1994 and my landlord wanted to rebuild his house. He wanted us to move out and started to demolish the shed in the backyard. He would never respect our rights as his tenants. I did complain to him but he did not take any notice. I finally complained to the Tenancy Board and they told me as there was no written contract between us, there was nothing they could do. There was a house for sale in my area. Every day I used to pass it, I prayed to God and Angels if I could buy this house. I was praying really hard to be able to buy it. I went to the agent. They said the house was $180,000. I went to several different banks and building societies but as I was a single self-employed mother, they all rejected my application. Finally, the Illawarra Credit Union was the last place I went to. The manager agreed to lend me $150,000 under special conditions. I needed another $15,000 for solicitor's fees, stamp duties and etc. I had already saved $15,000.

I went back to the agent and explained my situation and asked for $30,000 negotiation. He said maybe I might be able to get $5,000 or even $10,000 off the price of the house but there was no way the owner would agree to drop $30,000 from his asking price. I left my name and phone number with him and asked to contact me if the owner should change his mind. I went back home very disappointed; I was looking for a house around the $150,000 mark. There were none and I had my heart and soul set on that particular house. Whenever I prayed, I would see the house to be mine. I even had a vision of how it would look in the future. At the moment it was an old fibro home in a very poor condition. I prayed and waited patiently. Six months later the agent came to my door and said that he didn't know what I had done. That looked like I put a curse on the house because nobody had even made an inquiry about the house since I inspected it. Therefore, the owner was willing to give it to me for $150,000, as I was the only buyer. I replied it was the answer to my all prayer. How the house came to me was **another miracle of God**.

The sale went smoothly and on 20th, December, just before Christmas, we got the house key. My children and I were over the moon as our landlord was beginning to demolish a wall in the house while we were still living in. As our new house was in the same area we started to clean it up and to move some of our possessions over. The garage was not in any condition to be converted to my clinic. Therefore I went back to the bank manager and told him about the nature of my job. I explained if they would lend me another $20,000 to build my clinic, I could work and repay my loan. The bank agreed and I found the cheapest builder to build a 10 x 6 meters shed to be able to be divided by curtain for clients' privacy. The builder was working with his only labourer. My sons and I were his other labourers. I was an owner builder and I used to buy the materials on my three credit cards. The builder charged $20,000 for the shed and some repairs on the house and he also paid for some of the materials.

We started during Christmas holidays; we worked days and nights. The builder would leave late in the afternoon and my sons and I would continue up to 10 pm. Then they would go to sleep and I would continue up to 2 or 3 am. I cooked three meals for everybody every day plus I worked from my old clinic on the premises where my former landlord was already demolishing the house. Before the building was finished the builder started playing up, not coming and finally he said that there was not enough money for him to finish the work. There was only an oral contract between us, not a written one, but I kept all the copies of his pay cheques. I also had a video of his work. All his building tools were left on my premises. One early morning he came very quietly without my permission and started to pack up his tools into his car. All of a sudden I woke up with the noise. I went out and told him that he cannot take them as he has taken all my money without finishing the job. Everything, however, was already in his car and he said those were his tools. I was so desperate and feeling helpless; so I took his car key and throw it as far as I could. He found the key and went back to the car. I stood in front of his car and told him the only choice he had was to drive me over. My children were watching this and were trembling. Therefore he called the police. When police came I was crying my eyes out and telling them what this man had done to me; he had taken off with the money. The police said that I had to let him go and if I wanted to, I could take legal action against him. I had to let him go and I sat and cried for hours and hours. I took the legal action and after six months I won the case. The judge ruled that the builder should compensate me $50,000. But I got nothing as he announced bankruptcy. The electrical work was still left; some of the gyprocking, painting and tiling still had to be done. One of my clients' husband, who was an electrician, felt sorry for us and agreed to do the job for $2,500 and I could pay him in instalments. My oldest son and I finished the gyprocking together and my son did all the painting.

While the builder was still working for us, I had a letter from Prince Henry hospital for my operation on my knee. I had been suffering for the past 18 years and I was on a waiting list for the operation. Therefore I went for the operation by myself, as the pain was unbearable. I had the operation and they removed some glasses, sand and rotten flesh above my knee. The specialist came to see me after the operation. He showed me what they removed from my leg. He said that it was unbelievable that I could live with this for the past 18 years without going into my bloodstream and then into my heart, *another miracle of God*. He said that I had to stay in hospital for a week; and then I had to rest for the next six weeks. He continued I would not be able to walk for at list one week. At night I needed a bedpan. I rang the bell constantly and I was screaming to get a nurse to help me but no one came and I wet myself. I had to wait until the morning. The nurse who came to change the bedding asked me what happened and I explained to her. She replied "there was only me in the whole section and I had so many other emergencies to attend to last night". I was the only patient who did not have any visitors. One time during visiting hours when all other patients had visitors I was upset, crying and praying. I felt an Angel kiss my cheeks then I fell into the best most relaxing sleep.

The next night the same thing happened—I needed a bedpan and there was no response. This time I got out of bed and with all the difficulty I reached the toilet by myself. From then on, I did not ask for the bedpan any more. The doctor came for a visit and found me walking from the toilet to the bed in the morning. He told me off for not obeying his instructions. I replied that I did not want to wet myself again as there was not enough staff to attend to all the patients. I believed that I could continue to look after myself better at home. He said that he would give me a pair of crutches and insisted that I should use the crutches for at least six weeks. My oldest son picked me up from hospital and brought me home. Two days later, I started to work in a small part of the clinic which was not tiled yet. Then after, I was tiling the clinic up to 4 o'clock in the morning, even though I was still in excruciating pain. The business was blooming and people were coming to me from everywhere, which to me was *another miracle of God*. I managed to pay all my debts and also my monthly loan repayments. I gradually renovated my house and I bought a brand new car, too. I still had to see a doctor to check my operated knee every week and thankfully it was healing well.

One of my clients and her partner invited me for a coffee. When I went there one of their friends was already there. He was a divorced man with nine children; badly hurt, angry and depressed by his divorce, as it was not his choice. His wife had an affair with his best friend who was also married with 5 children. She ended up having another child to this man. So, because of that, two marriages were broken up and lives of 15 children were destroyed. The only feelings I had towards him been sorry for him. My client informed me that he was attracted to me and would like to date me, later on. I told my friend "No way, I have gone through so much pain and suffering and I could not even think about such a relationship. Even if he would be the best man, he still has nine children with all their problems. I do not mind helping him, any way I can but I do not want to get romantically involved with him". He came to me for a haircut shortly after. We were talking every time he came. He continued to come every two weeks and I was beginning to like him as I thought he is an innocent lovely man who had been hurt. He was a respected computer programmer who was working 3 jobs to look after his family as best as he could. I strongly felt his spirit around me. Every time I prayed and asked God and Angels to guide me, the message was "Marry him and save his soul". Therefore, it was an assignment from God, which, at the time, I thought it would be beneficial for me as well. He was financially ruined as most of his assets went to his wife and children. The little bit of money that he was awarded was spent on legal fees for the access of his five youngest children. He lost all the money and still had no access to his youngest children after two years. He was drinking heavily to cover up his pain for all his loss but he stopped drinking and smoking and was very happy to have me in his life. He was constantly praising me and calling me his goddess. We got married after four months. All he had was a little bit of money from his superannuation which he bought me a wedding ring and we went for one week honeymoon. One week before our marriage we went to attend to one of his son's graduations with two of his other sons and a nephew. The graduation was held in another state. We had a car accident on the way back. It was raining and I was driving within the speed limit. A truck that was driving in the opposite direction blinded me and I went off the road. The car rolled over a couple of times and landed on the roof. As I felt out of control with the car, I passed out. I felt that I was in a beautiful light with God and

Angels. I said to God "God, I just wanted to have some nice time in my life. It is not fair to take me now". The next thing I remember was a police officer telling me to give him my hand to get me out of the car. I'd ended up actually sitting on top of the steering wheel while I was wearing a seatbelt; the fact I can't explain to this year. My future husband and the three boys were asleep in the car and did not have any recollection of the accident. They were totally unharmed. I was taken to hospital for observation. I was bruised all over my body and my toes were injured. I was told that I would need surgery on them later on. The car was totally written off. My son hired a car and picked us up; four days after the accident we got married. I had lots of problems with my two sons to accept that marriage. They were very protective of me and it was hard for them to accept my marriage because of our background culture. I strongly believe that it was my destiny and nobody could have stopped that marriage. I was enjoying every minute of my breathing and living. We went to North Folk Island for our honeymoon, which was my husband's choice.

I could feel and even see lots of unhappy spirits who had been killed unfairly in the past, at the first night when we got there. I would just pray for them and asked them to leave. Then I asked God and Angels to show me if there was any past life between my husband and myself. I was shown that we had two past lives together. One of those was an English officer who was married to me and was sent to North Folk Island to do his duty. So, lots of those unhappy spirits were angry with him; they would harm him if they could to revenge the past injustices. We went to different places and everywhere I went I could see those spirits. They would tell me their life story. When I would talk to people who were living on North Folk Island, they would confirm what the spirits told me in a couple of times.

One day we drove up to the mountain on which you could see the whole island. I could see all these spirits and that was the strongest contact I had ever had. I went to the car and asked my husband to leave. I could see the spirits trying to push him off the mountain, as they were angry with him. But he was not aware of those spirits. Actually I was the one who could see them and he was really enjoying himself. Finally I screamed at him and he came down. We were the last car up there and everyone else had already gone, as it was getting dark. While we were driving off the mountain, we could see a flashing light from the mountain which had absolutely no electricity connection. My husband saw that and he wanted to go back and check it out. I had a feeling the spirits wanted to get him back there. I persuaded him not to go. I explained all the things that were happening to us ever since we arrived on the Island. He believed it a little but was not convinced, as he could not understand it. We came back after a week and I was so glad to get out alive of there. Three days after arriving home, we had to go to the court in relation to a charge from his ex wife. This went on for about six months and at the end, he had to serve weekend detention for a year. The judge announced "I am so sorry to sentence you as the jury are not allowed to hear your side of the story and I am the only one who is aware of the circumstances surrounding this case". When we came home, I went to the backyard, screamed and talked to God for the injustice. I had to take him every Friday night to the detention centre and pick him up on Sunday afternoons. I realised that he was so scared and his pride was crushed as well. He started drinking heavily again and became a totally different man from the one whom I married.

I tried to understand and give him the right to be the way he was; but he became worse and worse and many times, he punished me for what his ex wife had done to him. I started to feel very sad again; my happiness only lasted six months. The more I tried to help him the more he negatively reacted toward me. He generalised all women as f... b... and had no respect for any females. I had to take care of my life in every way plus taking care of an angry and bitter man. We appealed the sentence with the help of one of my friends' husband, who was in the legal system, as we had no money to pay other legal fees. We won the case but he had already done six months of detention. They informed us that we could sue the legal system as his sentence was quashed but we decided against it as we already went through too much. The good thing was that his name and reputation were cleared. I tried to teach him how to successfully run a small business and enrolled him in some short natural therapy courses. But he did not show any interest in that field. He continued to be angry and revengeful more than ever. He would be drinking heavily and staying out with his mates who were in the same situation. I did not feel like a married woman as my husband was never with me. I asked him that he should be spending time with his wife at home as a married man after all I have done for him. His answer was "I do as I like"!

Even though I was not happy with that situation, I continued living. This marriage was completely my choice and I was feeling a total failure. That was why I kept everything to myself and let him be. My children and I were very nice to all his children and his family. I welcomed his children as my children but his four oldest children were very bitter, angry, lost and hurt as their mother left them behind and took the other six with her and moved interstate. They were rebelling and causing trouble all the time, and not responding to my kindness.

My husband's mother, who was a very strict Catholic, also did not accept me as her daughter-in-law. She always said that his ex-wife, who crucified him, was her daughter-in-law forever. She believed that he should never get married, while my husband and his ex-wife were legally divorced. She had her marriage annulled by the Catholic Church, changed her and the youngest six children's surname and totally destroyed his life. She also hated her mother-in-law. However, my husband's mother didn't acknowledge my marriage considering all the good things I'd done for her son and his family to that day. She always made me upset by mentioning that his ex-wife was her only daughter-in-law. She did not come to our wedding and would totally ignore me and walk away every time she saw me. Even when we were in the court to support my husband, she acted in the same way.

The day my husband was suppose to go to jail all his family came to support him but not his mother. I decided to go to her house, break that barrier and bring her to my house for her son's sake.

I went to the house; she opened the door and turned her face away from me as usual. I told her that I had done nothing wrong to her and I loved her. I continued that I would be most glad if she would come for her son's happiness before he went to jail. She shut the door in my face but after about one hour she did come to my house. She would start to acknowledge me by saying Hello to me but she still would not acknowledge me as her daughter-in-law after that. On the other hand my father-in-law was a very loving, caring and gentle man who welcomed me from the beginning. He was very grateful for all I did for his son. I loved him like a father, as he was always nice to me even though he was a very sick man. He did everything to please his wife and would never do anything to upset or hurt her. He never complained and always smiled; he passed away only recently.

What I could see in my husband was a total copy of his mother who would not care about anybody's opinion. What they believed was right was right—no question asked. And I could see the same similarities in her other two sons. I could say that they were very loving and caring toward other people but not their own family. My husband was the favourite of everyone who knows him, as he would do anything for anyone but not for his family. When I asked him to do something for me it would take ages. When I complained that he should also help me the same as helping other people, he would reply, "You are not the priority".

I had to have operation on all my toes due to my recent car accident as I was still in a lot of pain. After that I had to walk with frame and then on crutches. For the first six weeks I needed constant help and my husband was the only available person but he was not caring and helpful, at all. Every time I cried and helplessly asked for his help he did not pay any attention to me. I mostly managed with the frame to look after myself. I had a phone call from my youngest brother in England that he was not feeling well and he was going through divorce. Even though my financial circumstances were not good, I bought tickets with my credit cards and went to England with my husband and my daughter. I saw my brother for the first time after 19 years. We stayed for six weeks to look after him and his family that made a big change in his health and wellbeing. We came back while I still had problems with my toes. My surgeon informed me that I would need another operation. I had my second operation at the end of October that only involved two toes on each foot. Therefore I could walk with special shoes and I had six weeks off work. Therefore I decided to do some post graduate studies in England and also to give me and my husband a little bit of space to work out our marriage. After six weeks, when I came back nothing had changed; he was even worse.

He did not have any respect for women in general. He would always say nasty jokes about women and call my daughter and me using rude words. I tried all my counselling and therapeutic knowledge on him but there was no avail. I decided to go on a retreat interstate with him hoping to sort out his problems. We stayed for a week and while we were there he was reasonably calm. When we came out of the retreat I was hoping he would stay the same. Within a short time, he stopped in a pub and had some beer. We continued driving and he started his abusive language again! I realised that it was only a waste of time and money. During the trip, I had a phone call from my son who was very angry and upset. One of my husband's sons came to our door and abused and threatened my teenage daughter for a very minor issue. My sons had found my daughter at home in a stage of shock and they were very upset. I tried to calm them down and asked them for taking care of their sister until my arrival. When I explained the situation to my husband, instead of acting like a caring step father he went ballistic. He started swearing at me and calling my daughter stupid f… b…; he continued that she deserved it and that my sons should be quiet as his sons can become so violent and "fix them up". He was driving like a maniac and I was afraid that we would have an accident. It did not matter how much I begged, cried and tried to calm him down; he would not listen. When we arrived home I hugged my children, tried to calm them down and did not say about his response to that situation. But he did; he told my daughter that it was her fault and she deserved it all and then he walked out. That was the end of relationship between my children and his children. He never accepted that his son had no right to behave towards my daughter the way he did. I still kept quiet to keep my marriage. I was really feeling ashamed of getting divorced again.

My husband and my daughter were constantly clashing as he was forceful and abusive. I constantly had to be the peacemaker between them. I prayed hard for him to find a job as I thought working might give him some independency and make our life better. He got a job in another city with a good salary but he had to drive up and down daily. After a while, he decided to get a room in that city, stay there during the week and come home only for weekends. The situation was a bit better because we did not see each other that much. But he started not coming home even on weekends and even when he came on a weekend, he would spend most of his time with his single friends or his children. I did not mind him spending any time or money on his children but I wanted him to spend some time with me instead of his single friends. I even had to beg him to have breakfast on a Sunday with me. So, we started to grow more and more apart as it was only me who worked on this marriage. He would only occasionally come home on a weekend and sometime it would be 4 am! I decided to keep myself busy with my work, studying and my children and just let him be to keep the marriage, as I was ashamed of getting a divorce. The more I compromised the more he took advantage of the situation, continued being aggressive and abusive. I decided to do a university degree in science, majoring in nutrition.

When I informed him he made fun of me and said "You are 50! Do you think you have the brain for it?" It hurt me but it would not deter me from my goal. I started it as a full time student while I was running the business and household, too. It was very hard to go back to university as the education system was totally different and very hard for me to adapt. The first year was the hardest; the student advisory board and also two of the lecturers reminded me that I was 50 years old and science degree is very hard. They said that I would be better to do a psychology degree or give up. But their opinion made me even more determined to succeed. I finished my degree in three years and received an apology from my husband and others who doubted me.

At the end of the first year of university I separated from my husband as I could not deal with his behaviour anymore. I needed to have peace of mind and get my strength back. Six months later, he decided to divorce as he wanted his freedom without any responsibilities. I asked him to give our marriage another chance by trying to change his ways and attitude if he would like. The next day we went out for a dinner and I was hoping for a good answer. On the way back home, however, he said that he really wanted to end the marriage and get a divorce. That devastated me; I got out of the car and started walking towards the park across our street while it was raining. I was crying, talking to God and walking in the rain. I reached the front of a Catholic church in our street where he goes every Sunday. I was crying and talking to the statue of Mary and asking Jesus and Mary for assistance in reconciliation of our marriage. My husband was following me, as he had never seen me in that state. He kept telling me to calm down and go home because I was soaking wet. Finally, I went back home and cried and cried; and within a week he brought the divorce papers for me to sign. He said that this was the best thing for both of us. It was the hardest time of my life, as I felt so guilty and ashamed. That marriage, that was my choice against all the wishes of my family, had failed.

For a while I even started to doubt myself that there must be something wrong with me; all my three marriages failed. Each of them started with passion and love but ended up hurting me. It took me a long time to recover and accept that maybe marriage is not for me and I did not question and criticise my husbands or myself. I knew that if I stopped loving myself I would end up getting sick again. I continued with my life and I realised married or not married I had to be self reliant. He started to live his life like a single young man again and having fun and going on holidays with his friends. Two years after our divorce he came to me for help, as he was not feeling well. As a healer and a health practitioner, I started helping him and he is one of my patients until this day.

I do not keep grudge and I do not believe in hate and revenge. Even if my worst enemy should come to my door for help I do not refuse to help. I have a very good relationship with his whole family and during the year of his father's sickness, I supported his parents totally in every way. I was with his father when he took his last breath. My ex husband came to my graduation with a nice bunch of flowers and took my family and me for a celebration dinner in a nice restaurant and apologised for insulting me during my studies. My graduation day was the biggest victory and the happiest time in my life as I had to do it in the hardest way possible—building my house and my clinic, going through my marital problems and still I had to work to support myself and my family.

During the second year of my studies, I started to do some home renovation. My home loan was paid off and the house was a very old fibro house and needed lots of repairs. I got a loan on my equity and did an owner builder course. I employed builders and labourers to start on the renovations. When the house was finished, I knocked down the old clinic which was in a very bad condition as well. The new clinic was professionally built because of my lessons from the house experience. So, I had to deal with the building tradesmen, on top of all my other responsibilities as well. I provided morning and afternoon tea and lunch for all the tradesmen (about 10) every day to look after them. But they did not do the right thing and caused me so many problems. That could almost bankrupt me as the cost and time ended up being double to the original estimate. After finishing the house, I started working from a room in the house and rebuilding the clinic. The clinic was finished within five months in perfect time and cost. I contracted all the professional tradesmen and I did not feed them and was very firm. Finally, I started to work from my dream clinic. I strongly believe that finishing the buildings without losing everything was **another miracle of God**. I advertised the opening of my new clinic, which has six treatment rooms plus reception area and a seminar room. It functions as a "mini" retreat centre including a day spa. The clinic was really busy and I was managing to pay my loan and my expenses.

Soon after my graduation I became very sick which was due to all the toxins from building materials and also not getting enough rest. It took me three weeks to recover. During those three weeks I was so weak and tired that I could hardly get out of bed; I felt that I was going to die. I was praying and talking to God and Angels to save me and let me enjoy my dream house and clinic. After I recovered, I started working hard again. The clinic was busy; I also ran workshops and seminars locally and interstate. I used to go to Body Mind and Spirit Festival twice a year. The two workshops that I run were Angel Workshop and Energy Healing Workshop. I also wrote articles for different newspapers and magazines.

At the beginning of 2006 I had a phone call from my younger brother in England informing me that my mother was on her death bed. Within a week I went to England to help her. I started to treat her from the time I arrived. She was suffering from diabetes, had 2 bypass surgeries and she also ended up with emphysema. She was on morphine and lots of other medications. I treated her with all natural remedies and gave her therapy. Within a week she could sit up, stopped her morphine and reduced her insulin from 65 units to 25 units. My older brother who lives in USA came with his wife; my sister also came from Canada so it was a lovely family reunion after 20 years of separation. They stayed for two weeks and I stayed for six weeks. My mother was reasonable recovered and able to do her own things again. During this time, as I was helping my mother, it was also helpful for me to resolve some issues from my past. I realised that I had to accept my mother the way she was. I believe we can only change ourselves and accept and respect others as they are. We also need to release our judgment and as we are all different beings, respect and love everyone as they are. On the way back I spent some time with my sister's family in Canada and some time with my brother's family in USA. After being away for three months, I came back home. That put me in a bad financial situation as I had no income for those three months while I had all my expenses. That took another year for me to financially, emotionally and physically recover. I continued with my business and also enjoying time with my family.

My second son was living with a very nice, loving and caring girl for seven years but they ended up separating which caused by helping a married couple. The married woman left her husband for my son hoping that he would marry her, but that was not his intention. The result of that relationship was a baby girl who my son has never acknowledged as he felt betrayed and trapped by the mother. Soon after he met a very nice Persian woman and within a couple of months they were married. They are happily married and have a son together.

I used to go once a month and see my granddaughter without my son's knowledge. When the girl was about 2 years old I received a phone call from Department of Community Services (DOCS) regarding my granddaughter's welfare. They informed me that the three children had been removed from the mother, as she is an unfit mother. The two older kids were given to their father. They contacted my son regarding his daughter but he had told them that he would take her only on one condition; that he would have the sole custody of her. They said to me that they could not do that and offered me to get involved for her sake. I had to go to the Dept of Community Services and make arrangement to have my granddaughter on weekends and the mother would have her on weekdays. My son was present at that meeting, as well. He told me if I did accept this arrangement I would not be allowed to see him, his wife and his son. Even though that was heart breaking to make such a decision but I thought that my granddaughter needed my support and I had to deal with the heartache of not seeing my son and his family. This arrangement lasted for three years but it was always problematic because of the mother and her partners' behaviour.

My granddaughter told me that her Mum used to leave her alone and she had to walk to school by herself. It was painful to hear the things she had to go through with her mother. Even though it was heart breaking to hear that I kept quiet for my granddaughter's sake. The mother had settled down with a partner and had a baby girl with him. One day when I went to pick my granddaughter up the mother was not home and I could hear yelling, shouting and swearing from inside. I knocked on the door and my granddaughter opened the door. She was pale, scared and shaking. Before I could say anything, her mother's partner was yelling and asking who was at the door and as soon as he saw me he was shocked. I asked him if he was yelling at my granddaughter and asked where her mother was. He replied that he just came from work and he found my granddaughter trying to change the baby's nappy and she made a mass so he lost control and yelled at her. The mother arrived and as I was so upset, I complained how she could leave a 3-month-old baby with a five years old girl at home by herself. She did not like that and told me that I am interfering and that she was not going to allow me to see my granddaughter anymore. That was the last day I saw my granddaughter. I contacted DOCS about the arrangement I had through the Children Court and they said that I have to take a legal action to be able to see my granddaughter again. I sought legal advice and I found it impossible financially and mentally to legally fight for her. I tried to contact the mother to make some suitable arrangement to see my granddaughter but to no avail. Every night I prayed for all my children and others and cried my eyes out for my son and his family, especially my deserted granddaughter.

At the end of my working day, I usually came inside, danced for half an hour and then did some yoga as a part of my daily routine. One day, about two months after above story, I felt dizzy and hot in the head. I suspected a high blood pressure, which I'd never had. I checked my blood pressure with my professional monitor; it was 220/110. Nobody was home; I had a shower, lied down, meditated and took some of my natural remedies. I checked my blood pressure every hour. By midnight, my blood pressure was 240/120. I kept calm, took some more remedies and went peacefully to sleep. The next morning my blood pressure was 160/90. It went up during that day until the night reached again to 240/120. This time my daughter was at home and insisted on taking me to hospital. I went to emergency. It was hard to believe for doctor that I had such a high blood pressure. She said most of the home monitors are not accurate. After twice checking of my blood pressure, she said that it is impossible. Therefore they checked my heart by ECG and that was normal. They said that I had to stay overnight for observation since that was dangerous. I didn't want to stay there overnight, so I signed a release form, came home and continued treating myself. I was under observation of my GP for several tests to find the cause. The full check up was done three times during the three months and nothing was shown. My GP is a witness that on some occasions my blood pressure went as high as 260/150 that I felt I was dying. But I never had any fear and stayed calm the whole time. I checked everything based on my knowledge in medical and alternative medicine field; I contacted so many practitioners and experts in their field all around the world as well as; my GP did lots of observation and tests through himself and other specialist and no one could come up with a reasonable answer for my high blood pressure. In the meantime, I was taking lots of homeopathic, herbal and nutritional supplements plus other remedies for my condition.

One night I was praying, crying, talking to God and Angels and asking them to give me an answer as to what was happening to me. The answer was to have an X-ray of my whole mouth! As I did it, I found out massive infected teeth due to root canals that I had for the last 20 years. I made my decision, went to a dentist and had the 10 infected teeth extracted. I treated the infection and went through lots of pain and agony but my blood pressure dropped. Everything was fine and after three months with the help of all remedies and God and Angelic Kingdom, I recovered and my blood pressure went back to normal; ***another miracle of God***.

My son, his wife and their son started to visit me again after two years. My first husband has been contacting me for the past 5 years from time to time. He decided to come here to see the children and me but there were some immigration difficulties and he could not come. He is still in contact with me and has sent me some letters to show me that he has never stopped thinking about me even though he was married to someone else. He has never been a caring father and has not shown any interest in his children's life. I have no hard feelings against him and wish him all the very best. My second husband has been in touch with his daughter and me over all the time and showed interest in his daughter's life. Until this day he still loves me and thinking of reconciliation, but I cannot accept him ever again. I only respect him as the father of my daughter.

My mother came to visit me for the third time and she was not well. I thought that this would be our last visit and I might receive some motherly love as I have been waiting for it all my life. I was emotional but I quickly reminded myself that was who she was. In fact, she was worse than ever and in many occasions I was close to tears. I looked after her in every way and she had the best time during the three months staying in Australia. At the end she said, "You have become an Angel yourself". I could not believe how I tolerated all her selfishness, hatred and bitterness. I realised how I have changed for the better by giving her unconditional love and accepting the fact she would not change.

When my mother went back to England, she lost some jewellery and she was accusing me of taking them. Because of that, every time I called her, I got an abusive conversation and on many occasions she hanged up on me. Therefore, I stopped calling her and only through my brother I found out about her health. After three months she went back to Iran to visit her family and friends. She still had her own luxury home and servants over there. She had a massive stroke there; she became paralysed on one side. I have been talking to her since then. Unfortunately, after two years her condition has not improved. She has been talking to me lovingly and asking me for forgiveness. I was always wishing for a loving and caring mother who I never had and it happened after this incident. She has spent $100,000 on her condition and there is no improvement. My brother moved her back to England after being in Iran for 8 Months; he was hoping that the Medical system in UK would help her condition. This shows that no one can be proud of his or her power, money or status. I also believe that we should never wish anything bad upon any one, as it will, come back to us. My mother would wish upon people who she disliked, to be end up paralysed in hospital. It happened to her after a massive stroke in the last three years of her life.

When my mother left within a few months, I had three men coming to my life that, I knew in the past. I was happy to hear from them and talk to them as a friend but not interested in marriage. I was working in my clinic and also doing lots of community work through Iranian community and was leading a very busy life.

Every Friday was our family day. I picked up my grandchildren; we played and danced together, I cooked and then my children came after work and we all had dinner together. My children became busier and grand kids got older, so I did not see them as much. All my happiness was to see them, be with them, but it was not the same for them. My daughter moved to Sydney, my second son went to USA and my oldest son was very busy with his company and his family. I started to fill very lonely; therefore I decided to accommodate an Iranian University student in my house; One girl who was doing her PhD and one boy who was studying bachelor degree. The boy moved out after 6 months, then a man who used to be a medical Dr in Iran and was doing his PhD in Medical informatics moved in. He was divorced and had a 10 years old son. I was working and looking after them plus lots of other student, which was part of my community work. After few months Dr and I became involved as we had strong connection. It was out of our power to stop this connection and finally we got married. I would never even imagine this marriage as our age difference (he is 20 years younger than me). I strongly believe that it was Gods will for us.

He is a man of every woman dream, ***another miracle of God***. We are Twin flame soul mate and we both thanking God for his wonderful gift. This is my life now. I am enjoying my work and my family and friends. I feel very contented. I enjoy my life to the fullest and I accept God's will or karma or destiny.

My oldest son did not approve my marriage and gave us very hard time and stop coming to my house. Therefore, I did not see him and my two grand children, but all my family and friends including my other son and daughter were very happy for me and gave us their blessing. My oldest son also accepts it after a year and has a good relationship with my husband.

I had a phone call from the mother of my 10 years old granddaughter. She had cancer and she would like me to see my granddaughter after a long time, which she previously stopped my visitation. I was over the moon and happy as my pray was finally answered and I could see my granddaughter. Sadly my granddaughter's mother passed away one year after.

I was calling my mother every second days and talk to her. She was suffering and asking God to take her. It was very painful to hear her in so much pain. I had a dream about my father, he said to me "your mother has suffered enough and I am going to take her." My mother passed away one week later. Her soul has completely cleared, as she went through lots of pain and suffering. I had funeral for her and could not stop crying and grieving for two weeks. I knew my mother was going to come back as my granddaughter. My daughter gave birth to a beautiful little girl, two weeks after my mother death. When I looked in to baby's eyes, I saw my mother's soul in her that shifted all my grief. My mother loved my daughter very much. I take care of the baby three days per week when my daughter goes to work.

I have come to the conclusion that we are born with certain destiny (karma). The best way to deal with life challenges is to accept it and work on ourselves. Stop blaming the family, the spouse, the society or etc. Acknowledge and discover yourself and work toward fulfilment. We are here to change ourselves, not others; to give love and respect to others and ourselves. Make life of a child as an example. When children fall down and hurt themselves, they get up and go. If they fight with together, they make peace immediately. They do not hold grudges. We have to try to be childlike; and also forgive and love everyone the same way we forgive and love our own children; and accept challenges whether good or bad. That is how I could go through my difficult life and survive.

Many nights, I would feel I have been taken somewhere when I slept. In couple of times I saw myself on the bed while I felt on the ceiling. I couldn't remember where I've been taken but I had so much spiritual knowledge in the next morning that I have never been aware of. I believe that I was taken to the spiritual world as I have written things that I had to look for their meanings. The following is one of those manuscripts.

## "God"; the universal life force

We all have an unlimited power within us which is a matter of understanding and learning to effectively use it. The universal law is pure energy. It has no way of knowing what you likes or dislikes. It accepts whatever thoughts, feelings and actions you project and unemotionally reflects them back to you in the form of events that you experience day to day. The universal law will give you anything you believe in as thoughts and feeling, no more and no less. Those people who are locked within the limitations of body and mind can only experience little spiritual growth. We are not our bodies, our emotions or our minds, we experience around us. We are an infinite part of the God's force using the physical form to experience spiritual development through a special teaching called daily life.

As you entered the earth through the birth you had a heroic mission within your consciousness—a goal. The nature of that goal is firmly written in the very deepest recess of the inner you. What you are today, no matter what you feel about yourself, is actually a part of that goal in various stage of completion. Your mind began recording events, thoughts and feelings from the time of your birth. Your heroic goal in life is to learn to love yourself and accept full cosmic responsibility for what you are. You cannot overcome weakness by fighting it or thinking your way out of it. You overcome weakness by leaving it behind you. This means that you become aware of the inner tendencies and you move yourself out for the slovenly ways of the collective unconscious into a discipline of power. From time to time, you may drift back but once you decide on the side of strength, the power of the God (universal law) will always be with you to varying degrees. It may seem as a battle but is the nature of your mission on the earth. This attachment, which you accepted at birth, is your main challenge in life and your spiritual goal is to step above it.

We experience our life through the five senses. We are taught what capacity those senses have. Yet, each of them has a dimension that is many times deeper than is normally perceived and those dimensions will open for you as you move toward them. Through feelings, you can enter into other worlds and heightened sense of feelings is a capacity you can learn to develop quite quickly.

Everything around you is energy; your body, your thought and the events of your life—each expresses energy. A part of that energy is perceivable through the five senses; you will become aware of the subtlety of energies around you. You will find that you can use your feelings to guide you through life. The universal law (God), as living spirit, is unlimited. This force is within you. Therefore, what you are is unlimited. The universal law is impartial and unemotional, it cannot discriminate. It would give you anything you believed in. Trying to fix your circumstances just physically or mentally will not work in the long term, because deep-rooted inconsistencies will continue to surface in your life in various guises. To overcome something once and for ever, you have to get in touch within yourself to discover the real causes of the disturbance. This process or discovery will allow you more energy, which can be used to create the things you want in your life.

# Patients have been healed by my treatment and healing hands

I believe the healing treats the emotional, mental and spiritual side of the patients and my extensive knowledge of alternative medicine helps the physical side of the patients. I have treated many patients from flu to cancer. I also have helped so many patients who had no hope of surviving. At the beginning of my healing for the first three years, I was not charging any money and only received what my clients were willing to pay. As a result I ended up going to social security to be able to survive; as I was doing lots of healing that was not bringing any income for me. Also, doing too many healings was draining me. Finally my GP advised me that this was a gift to me to give to people which is priceless. But I should charge for my time to survive. He also insisted that I should not do more than 10 healings in a week. I felt guilty to charge as it was a free gift from God and should be given free of charge to other people, but gradually I would come to terms with this concept. I still give healing and my services free of charge to the unfortunate poor people. Throughout the years of healing, I have been used and abused by many affluent people.

← The first patient who I healed was 30 yours old lady with bone cancer. Her sister was one of my patients who came to the clinic and asked me if I would go to the hospital and give healing to her dying sister—she was put on morphine and given just a short time to live as the cancer was already spread throughout her body and the doctors could not treat her. I went to hospital with her sister and started giving her healing. As I was giving the healing, my whole body was shaking and I started to talk to her with a different voice, telling her that she was healed and should stop the morphine and go home. I tried so hard not to say that but it was out of my control. I finished the healing and I went back home. The next day, her sister rang and informed me that after I left, her sister stopped the morphine and released herself against all the family's wishes and came home. She asked me to go to the sister's place and continue treating her. I was going to her house for a couple of weeks, giving her healing and also some alternative remedies. Within three months, she was cancer free after all the doctors' observations. She has yearly checkups until this day and there is no sign of her cancer. She is very healthy and has 3 children, ***another miracle of God***.

← I had a 36 years old lady with a chronic back pain who had couple of metal plates inserted into her spine. She had to have implanted pain killer medicine as a result of broken screw and nothing could be done to fix it. She could hardly walk and wheelchair was her future. I treated her; she got rid of her pain killer implant and as she was recovering, another specialist could repair the snapped screw and she was not in pain and agony anymore. She is walking and living happy now, ***another miracle of God***.

← A mother of a six-year-old boy called me and booked for a facial treatment. As she walked to the clinic she stared at me and said "You might not believe this but I have been seeing you in my dreams many times. But you were wearing a white Indian sari with a message for me that to bring my sick son to you for healing". I was as surprised as she was and asked her what was wrong with her son. She told me that for the last 6 years they had taken him to every known specialist, doctors, alternative practitioners and etc. but no one had been able to help them. The father was an engineer and she was a nurse who did not believe in healing. After seeing me in her dream and coming to me, however, she became a believer. The young boy was uncontrollable to the degree if they would take their eyes off him he could burn the house down in a minute. He was under heavy sedation all the time and he could not go to normal school. The mother had to give up work to be able to constantly watch him. She brought her son to me with her husband. As I went to the boy to talk to him, he pushed me away with a horrible voice and said, "Don't touch me". He was a gorgeous boy like an angel but he had an evil spirit. I held him in my arms regardless him pushing me away. As I held him he just melted in my arms; and I started giving him healing. The parents were present in the room and saw the whole procedure. That little boy turned to an angel. He is a fine man who is now attending University, *another miracle of God*.

← A lady came to the clinic for a beauty treatment. As I started her treatment, I could see a spirit of a little girl around 5 years old in an angelic dress walking around my treatment bed. She wanted me to help her mother who was getting the treatment. It was very difficult for me to say anything as this lady was in my clinic just for some beauty treatment. But the spirit of the little girl would not let go. At the end of the treatment I started to explain to the mother that I am a medium and a healer and I could see the spirits of the deceased loved ones. Then I told her about her little girl; as I mentioned it, she started to cry her eyes out and telling me that she lost her 5 years old girl from leukaemia and since then she has not been able to cope. She was very depressed and even though she had another three children who needed her she was not able to accept the loss of her 5-year-old daughter. She came to the healing and getting connected to her daughter's spirit healed her wound. She could continue her life with acceptance of her daughter's loss as she knew that she was around her and was serving God and Angelic Kingdom, *another miracle of God*.

← A 42 years old lady came to me with a shoulder complaint, experiencing stabbing pain that she has had for over 5 years. The pain was so debilitating that she could not lift her arm. I was her last resort. She had already seen doctors, orthopaedic specialists, surgeons, physiotherapists and etc.; no one was able to help her. After only a few treatments, her shoulder "unlocked" and she was pain free.

She came to me 7 years later, this time with a chronic kidney failure. She had been on high blood pressure tablets for nearly 20 years. She was told that she would lose the function of her kidneys in less than 2 years and she would have to go on dialysis for the rest of her life, as she could not be even helped with a kidney transplant. She was given lots of medication; at one stage she was taking up to 15 tablets a day and on top of that she became very anaemic and had to give herself injections once a week. She lost over 20 kg in weight and was so fatigued, pale and weak. She was forced to give up work and spent most of her time in bed resting. I started treating her and now her kidneys are perfectly working.

She has got an unusual form of lymphoma as the side effect of all the medications she received, that I am treating now. Even the lymphoma is under control and since she was diagnosed with it 3 years ago, it's not become worse. She now enjoys a healthy and happy life and has lots of energy, *another miracle of God*.

← A lady brought his brother, a 40 years old gentleman to me. He was suffering from an unknown disease for a year. Medical field could not find a cause and he was only on painkillers and antidepressants. He told me that he was dying and no one knows why and if I would be able to heal him he would buy me a house. He was a very rich businessman from interstate and at the time I was living in a run-down fibro house that I was renting. I started giving him healing every day for 2 weeks. By the end of the 2 weeks he was back to life with no complaints, *another miracle of God*. The businessman brought me some flowers, a watch and a box of chocolate and I wished him all the best.

← A 55 years old gentleman came to my clinic. He was suffering from chronic unbearable headaches for 20 years and was treated by medical field. He could not work and his last hope for help was me. He told me that he was told by an orthodox priest in another state that a woman healer whose name started with "V" will heal him and therefore he started to search and after 2 years he found out about me. I started to give him healing and after six sessions his headache was gone. He is fine till now, *another miracle of God*. This man has sent me so many others, sick and unfortunate for healing.

← The above mentioned gentleman came to me 2 years later with a picture in his hand and asked me to send healing to his niece, a 23 years old girl with cancer who lived in United States. I told him that I have never done such a thing before, but I would try my best and sent healing to the picture of that girl. Three months later he came to the clinic with an envelope, which contained some money and a Thank You card and informed me that the girl was totally healed and cancer free, ***another miracle of God***. This was my first absent healing and I have done hundreds absent healings since that time.

← A 60 years old gentleman who has been suffered with a constant stabbing pain in his heart for 30 years came to me as his last hope. Medical field could not find a reason and his heart was healthy. He could not live a normal life and had his hand over his heart all the time. He only had one session of healing and his heart pain was gone, ***another miracle of God***. However, his heart pain transferred to me and I could not get out of bed; it took me 2 weeks to recover. I had to call my GP and explain the situation; he said that he hoped I charged him $1,000 as I would not be able to do any healing for the next 6 weeks. I replied he gave me $20 while he was a very rich man.

← A 21 years old gentleman who suffered with fear, anxiety and nervous disorder for 11 years came to me. Even the strongest antidepressants and sleeping tablets could not help his condition. He had medical professional help and he also had help from priests as he was suffering of an unusual circumstances. He showed me a stabbing scar that ran from his sternum to his navel and it was not from any surgery. He explained that in his dream, which was so real, he saw devil stabbing him exactly where he had his scar when he was 10 years old. Since then he has been sick and no one has been able to help him. I performed a special healing for his case. He had three sessions of healing and he was healed. His scar is still there but he is not fearful anymore, ***another miracle of God***.

← A 6 years old little girl was suffered from cancerous tumour in her foot and lower leg. Medical field decided to amputate her leg and the mother decided to seek alternative medicine and therapy before making final decision on amputation. She had six healing sessions plus some natural supplements and her tumour started to shrink. The little girl was so happy and she drew me as an Angel. She continued with my treatment and within 4 months, there was no sign of any tumour in her leg, ***another miracle of God***.

← A 7 years old little girl who was losing her eyesight and hearing came to me. The medical field diagnosis was that she was born with it and that she will eventually be deaf and blind. The little girl and her mother were devastated and desperate for help. After three healing sessions and some natural remedies her eyesight and hearing was perfect, ***another miracle of God***. She also did a drawing of me as an Angel.

← A lady in her early thirties came to me for beauty treatment as I was advertised in beauty section of the Yellow Pages. While I was working on her face she was looking at me like someone that she knew. She burst into tears and said to me "I have seen you in my dream. I was guided to come to you for help, but I'm not sure why". I explained to her about my healing power and I believed the spirit of her 10-year-old son has been guiding her to me for help, as the mother was depressed. She came for healing and after 6 sessions she was recovered, looked at life differently and found peace, ***another miracle of God***.

← A 24 years old lady was suffering from depression to the extent that she was contemplating suicide. She came to my clinic; as she arrived and saw the angel statues and pictures everywhere she burst into tears. She said that her 3 years old daughter brought the Yellow Pages to her, opened on the page "Beauty" and showed her my ad and told her "Mummy, go to the Angel". I welcomed her in my arms and helped her with healing and therapy that made her a different person up to this day. She is living happily with her little girl without depression, ***another miracle of God***.

← A 40 years old lady came to me for help. She had been trying to have a child and spent a fortune on many medical treatments but failed I treated her with my healing and natural therapy and within four months she fell pregnant. She has two beautiful boys who are now around 9 and 10 years of age, ***another miracle of God***.

← A 28 years old nurse came to me for help. She had been trying to have a child for the last 8 years and sought medical advices which was not successful I treated her with healing and natural remedies and within 6 months she fell pregnant.

Her first son was born with some complications, which the doctors did not expect the baby to survive. She called me from hospital, crying and asking me to send healing to her baby boy. I promised to try my best. I prayed and sent her and her baby all my love and healing. The next day she called me and said "God bless you! Thank you so much. The baby is fine and there is nothing wrong with him. As soon as I get out of hospital I will bring him to you." She has now 2 teenage boys and both are fine, *another miracle of God*.

← A lady in her mid thirties walked into my clinic looking lost and did not know what she was doing there. I asked her "How can I help you?" She replied "Where am I? What is this place?" I could feel her pain and could see the Angels who brought her to my clinic. I took her to my healing room and explained to her about my work and myself. She started crying; she said that she lost her parents and her husband within 4 months, and that she was an only child and she had no children of her own. She felt so empty and decided to come to my city from interstate to go to the seaside and drown herself. She parked her car there and she did not know how she ended up at my clinic. I told her "The Angels brought you here for help", *another miracle of God*. I gave her healing and with all my assistance and God and Angels' help, she is doing lots of voluntary work. She is in peace by accepting God's will after experiencing miracle by herself.

← A 50 years old diabetic gentleman, whose leg was supposed to be amputated due to gangrene, came to me for help. I treated him with healing and lots of natural remedies on daily basis. He promised me that if I saved his leg he would give me half of his wages, as he was a wealthy man. After 3 months of intensive treatment he was totally cured and his leg was saved. He went back to work, *another miracle of God*. I was only paid my fee even though I spent double time on him than my other patients.

← A 38 years old lady who suffered from anorexia and nervous disorder came to me for help as she was badly deteriorating. I treated her with twice a week healing and natural remedies. From the first healing, she could eat little bit of food. On some occasions she told me that in the middle of the night she would feel she was starving to death. She would feel me at her side feeding her and at the same time I would feel that I was going over to help her. After 3 months she was a normal person who could eat and enjoy her life, *another miracle of God*.

← A 25 years old disabled gentleman was brought to me for help. He had a stroke as a result of vaccination at the age of 2 that totally disabled him. He could not walk or talk. He was under lots of medication; he also suffered with epilepsy, which the medical field decided to remove a part of his brain to stop the epileptic fits. He was worse after the operation and was traumatised by it. I started to treat him with my healing and some natural remedies and within the second week, when he came to the clinic, he would be smiling and happy to see me and trust me. I continued my work and he became a peaceful and happy man. His parents were happy and also sad as they were thinking they should have brought him to me before the operation. I had to work on his parents regarding their guilty conscience and at the end they were happy as he had some improvement, *another miracle of God*.

← A 55 years old businessman was brought to me with excruciating pain in his lower back that had put him into bed for 2 weeks. The doctors' observation was that he had three dislocated lumbar discs and he was supposed to have surgery the following week. The doctors warned him that there is only a 60% chance that the operation would be successful and he could end up in a wheelchair. He walked to the clinic with the help of his wife and he could not bend at all. By the end of the first treatment he could put his shoes back on himself and walk without help. After the second treatment he went to see his doctor and asked for another X-ray before his operation. The operation was cancelled as they could not find any dislocated discs and he continued his treatment. He could start working within two weeks, ***another miracle of God***. He has sent at least 50 patients to me by explaining his story.

← A 50 years old clinical psychologist came to me for help. She was not able to practice as a result of her condition. She had one year of psychotherapy but it did not make any changes in her condition. When I started her healing I saw the spirit of a deceased young woman around her who wanted to communicate with her through me. As soon as I mentioned about the spirit to her, she started to cry and said "Thanks God. I am not mad. You can see her too." Then she said they bought a beautiful mansion that was half finished. The previous owner's wife had cancer and passed away. Therefore the husband could not stay in the house without her and put the house for sale. She said they were still in the process of finishing building the house. But every time she would make a decision regarding design or colour, the spirit would appear to her and overrule her decision which was affecting her, her husband and the builder; as she would always change her mind according to the wishes of the spirit. All these events made her feel very sick. It was affecting her work as well. I told her the spirit was very sorry to scare and upset her to the extent that she got so sick. All she wanted was to finish the house in the way she wanted, as this was her dream house. The lady agreed to finish the house in the way she wanted. When the house was finished, I went to the house and did a special ceremony to help her to leave peaceful. She left and the new owners are living in their new house in peace, ***another miracle of God***.

← The same lady came back after 2 years telling me they have lots of problems in the house and she feels that this time there is another spirit disturbance. Her husband also was saying that he could also feel and hear the spirit's presence. I could feel from them that there were spirits of an Aboriginal family who were burnt on that land over 200 years ago and never left the land. They were angry; that was why everyone who bought that land faced problems. They were not in the house as they lived on the land. I had to go back to their place for another ceremony to send the spirits to light in peace. There was a space in the garden where nothing would grow and no one could understand why. I saw the Aboriginal family sitting in that spot. I convinced them to leave as they cannot revenge innocent people and they have to accept God's will; who ever wronged them would eventually pay for it by their Karma, *another miracle of God.*

← A 35 years old university lecturer came with a severe allergy in her scalp and face. Her face was so swollen that her eyes were almost invisible and her scalp was full of infected sores. She said that she had tried all the medical treatments and nothing helped her; she was not able to live a normal life, as she could not even sleep lying down. I started her treatment with the healing and natural therapy remedies. The swelling was reduced within 24 hours and she was totally healed after only 6 treatments and up to this day, she is my patient. She would not consider the use of medical assistance even though she was a person who did not have faith in natural therapy, *another miracle of God.*

← A mother came to me with an 8-year-old boy who was very depressed and suicidal. She had tried all the possible way in medical field and alternative medicine but no one had been able to help his situation. From the time he could talk, he had been telling his parents that he wants to die. He would not play with any children; and it did not matter what the parents did to make him happy, nothing worked. The mother brought him to me as the last hope for help. I started him with a healing. The first thing I felt was about his grandfather who suicided and his spirit was reincarnated into this little boy. I asked the mother if her father committed suicide. She cried and said he did and she could not believe that I had that information. I explained as a healer I received this information and that was the cause of her son's problem. I gave the boy couple of session of healing and some remedies. This boy became a happy boy with a normal life and the mother's belief changed through this procedure, *another miracle of God.*

← A 40 years old lady came for healing, as she was heartbroken after her 18-year-old relationship ended. She was very depressed and gave up any hope of further relationships. She was a very tall lady. As I connected with her I could see a lovely man who had been married to her but he was short and bold. The angels gave me the message for her that she is going to meet this man very soon and they will get married in less than a year. Even though she might not be physically attracted to him, but he is her soul mate who would love and adore her. When I mentioned this to her she strongly responded "Never! I hate short and bold men. Even if I meet him I will say goodbye at the first meeting." She came back after three months, smiling and telling me that everything happened as predicated by the Angels during the healing session. She met the bold and short man a week later and it did not matter how hard she tried to avoid, he was still very nice to her; she changed her mind and accepted him. She was engaged to him and she loved him deeply, ***another miracle of God***.

← A 23 years old lady came to me for healing. Her fiancé was with her, about 25 years old. As I started the healing, the Angels wanted me to warn this girl about her fiancé. I tried very hard not to say anything but the Angels took over me and delivered the message that was to keep away from this man, as he is dangerous and he could kill her. The girl came out of the session and said to me "Thank you very much. I did not come here to pay you and hear this nonsense". She walked out of my clinic. I asked the Angels why they would do this to me. They answered "We gave her the warning but it is up to her to believe or not." Two years later she came to my clinic with a 5 months old girl in her arms and said "Will you forgive me for not believing you and being rude to you?" She started to cry and explained that they started to live together. He was a psycho; he was bashing her all the time, even throughout her pregnancy. One day he hit her so hard that she was unconscious; he left as he thought she was dead. A neighbour took her to hospital and the police was looking for him. But there was no sign of him. And then she wanted me to help her and her little girl as she was in a very bad mental state and the medication was not helping her or her daughter. The little girl was hurting herself by hitting her head on the floor or the wall.

I started to give them both healing and remedies and now, whenever she comes for a session she has a list of questions for Angels. She is now married and has a son and managing her life very well, *another miracle of God*.

← A 30 years old married lady came to me with a skin problem. She and her husband were both highly educated and seemed very nice. But every time I was working on her skin, the Angels were showing me the danger she was in with her husband that I could not imagine. During the time of her treatment, I suggested her to have some healing as part of her treatment and I gave her the message from the Angels. She burst into tears with fear and told me "Please don't say anything. Yes, he is abusive, verbally and physically, but I am scared of him as he has said many times if I say anything to anybody, he would kill me". The Angels promised that she would be saved very soon from this painful relationship. After a year she came back for healing and told me what happened. She said one day, as she was badly bashed by him and totally unconscious, he left home. Luckily, her brother found her and took her to a hospital. She was in coma for 5 months but she made it and finally everything came out. He was charged and moved interstate and she was practising spirituality. She was sure that she was back to life miraculously. Later on she met a lovely man whom she married, *another miracle of God*.

← A 32 years old friend came to me for healing. She was very depressed and unhappy due to the breakup of her recent relationship. She loved this man very much but he went back to his previous girlfriend who was a beautiful model and she had no hope to compete with her. During the healing session I received a message that within less than a year he would come back to her, and he would be her husband within less than 2 years; He is her soul mate. She left the clinic telling me "Thank you for being nice to me but I don't think so. This is a fairy tale." I did not hear from her for about nine months and every time I rang she did not respond very well. She rang me and said that he sent her some flowers and asked her to go out on a date. Everything came true as the Angels said.

She became engaged couple of months later and married within less than 2 years. They are happily married and have a little girl, ***another miracle of God.***

← A very good friend of mine came for healing as she was going through some rough time. When I connected with her during the healing session the message was "Get away from this dangerous man. You are not safe with him." As I delivered the message my friend did not respond well and said "Thanks for your concern, but we love each other and I don't think he is dangerous. He is a psychiatric nurse and a loving and caring man." I told her that I was just delivering the message. She did not come back for another healing session but what the Angels had said started to happen. He was so nasty and abusive toward her; even started hitting her. She ended up getting an AVO against him, as he would not leave her alone. One day I was having dinner with her; as we came out, he attacked her in front of me, slapped her and threatened her that he would kill her. My friend ended up selling her unit and moved back to her parents place. She even moved out of the state for a couple of years and she became a recluse and told me "I am 40 and I accept that I will be by myself for ever as I have had so many bad relationships. I will be an auntie to your children". I asked her to come for another healing session. The Angels' message for her was that she is going to meet a lovely man who has been in a similar situation as her and is her soul mate. When they met they would be married within a year. She smiled and said "Thanks for being nice to me", but she did not believe same as the others. A few weeks later, she met somebody, moved back here and they've got married within a year. She said to me "He is that nice that he was worth waiting for all these years", ***another miracle of God.***

← A 16-year-old girl brought to me as she was going through a difficult time in her life. When she walked into the clinic she was wearing a black dress and her hair was black with yellow, blue, purple and red highlights. She had black nail polish and lipstick and eye make up with lots of jewellery symbolising devil. I asked her "Can I help you?" and she responded in a nasty way "Don't touch me!" She lied down on my healing bed at the request of her mother and aunt. She said that she didn't believe in God and Angels. The only way she would stop being who she was at that time, was to see an Angel herself without my touch. I started to pray and asked Arch Angel Michael to help this girl and bring her back to God and Angelic Kingdom. She started to see Arch Angel Michael and communicate with him. By the end of the session she was a beautiful and peaceful young girl. I said "Welcome back to God's Kingdom", as she was communicating with God and Angels as a little girl. But because of her abuse by a stepfather she had turned back on God. They came back the following week for another healing session. She had her hair back to her normal colour, wearing no makeup or nail polish and no jewellery; only a cross on her neck. Her mother said t that when they left my clinic and even before they reached the end of my drive way, she took all her jewellery off and asked her mother to put them in the bin. When she got home she put a colour over her hair and wiped off all her makeup. The girl was very happy and apologised for her attitude towards me. She informed me that she is connected with the Angels and she showed me some Angelic poems. She attended my Angelic workshop and she read some of her poems to the other participants. Now she is a social worker and helps lots of teenagers, *another miracle of God*.

← A 33 years old lady came to me with her back, shoulder and neck problem as well as chronic asthma. I treated her with healing and natural remedies. After her 40th birthday she collapsed at work and was taken to hospital for medical observation. She was having 50-60 fits a day. She stayed in hospital for a week and then she was transferred to another hospital for a specialist treatment. She was sent home after 2 weeks as they could not find any reason for her fits and told her to rest. I started to treat her with my healing and the natural remedies. Her fits reduced to 2 per day on the first week and twice a week during the second week; and 1 in the third week and no more after that. She could do her normal house duties after 2 months, *another miracle of God*.

← The above lady asked me to give healing to her 11 years old dog, which had cancer and was supposed to be put down. I said that I did not know if the healing would work on animals, as I have never done it previously. I went to her house and saw the dog. He was a very big dog, which I was scared of (as I had been bitten by a big dog when I was a young girl). The minute the dog saw me, he laid down at my feet. I put my hand on him and gave him some natural remedies and the dog lived cancer free for another 7 years, *another miracle of God*.

← A 30 years old lady had bladder functioning problem after giving birth to her first child in hospital. She had to leave the hospital with catheter bag because after doing all the medical tests, they could not find any reason for her condition. They did not know how long she would have to live with that condition. She came to me, terrified and very depressed. I started to treat her with natural remedies and healing. After the first month the use of the catheter was reduced and after three months she walked into the clinic and gave me a hug with a smile and happy face. She said she did not use the catheter at all and she was back to normal, *another miracle of God.*

← A 63 years old lady was suffering from severe end stage emphysema and was given three months to live. After one year of treating, her lungs were 50% better and she was functioning normal and even back to work place and enjoying being a grandmother, *another miracle of God*.

← A 52 years old gentleman was suffering from massive skin eruptions with infections, drug induced lupus and diabetes and gangrene from knee down to the toes. After four months treating him as a whole, his gangrene improved, his diabetes and lupus were controlled and he was not taking any medications and was able to back to work, *another miracle of God.*

All of the above mentioned cases are only a small sample of my many varied cases that I have helped with the help of God and Angelic Kingdom. I believe there is no disease or disorder that cannot be healed. We all have the healing power within us and with the right assistance the healing will occur. The affirmation, which was given to me by Angels and healed my enlarged heart, was ***I forgive, respect, accept and love myself and others.*** These Angelic affirmations came to me to help me deal with challenges and difficulties I have faced in my life.

# Angelic affirmations

*I am now releasing all issues related to past, present and future in
life.*
*I am now releasing all pain, fear, anger, ego, guilt, hatred, jealousy,*
*Stress, anxiety, worries, doubt, sadness, sickness,*
*Frustration, judgement and all negative emotion and thought*
*From my body, mind, emotion and spirit*
*I forgive, respect, accept and love others and myself.*
*I see, hear, think and feel with joy and love.*
*I accept the process of life.*
*I am safe and secure at all times.*
*I am at peace with others and myself.*
*I am immortal, eternal, universal and infinite.*
*I am what I am, and what I am has beauty and strength.*
*I love and approve of others and myself.*
*I am patient, I am strong.*
*I am happy, healthy and peaceful.*
*I am young and attractive.*
*I am fit and slender.*
*I am wise and intelligent.*
*I am successful and powerful in every aspect of my life*
*Without harming others or myself*
*I am totally protected by divine love from all negative influences.*
*I trust God and the Angelic Kingdom.*
*God is love and love is God.*
*I thank God for my health each day.*
*I smile and am cheerful every day and night.*
*I remind myself to be always honest to myself and others.*
*I witness God to be kind to people and never judgemental.*
*I keep secrets told to me by others confidential.*
*I improve myself everyday in every way I can.*
*I promise to love and respect people as they are.*
*I lighten my soul with knowledge and wisdom.*

*I sweeten my life with laughter and happiness.*
*I consider my work as a type of meditation.*
*I accept God's will as the path of my life.*
*I am patient and strong enough to deal with all of life's challenges.*
*I rob myself to help others not rob others to help myself.*
*I have unconditional love for myself and others.*
*I love God with faith not fear.*
*I am immortal, eternal, universal and infinite.*
*I see, hear, think and feel with joy and love.*

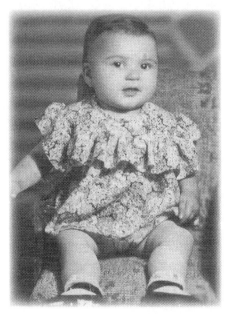

Victoria, 6 months old, 11 kg

Victoria with her parents

Victoria, 10 years old

Victoria, 12 years old

Victoria, 13 years old

Victoria, 15 years old

Victoria, 16 years old

Victoria, 17 years old

Victoria, 18 years old

1969, First marriage

1979, Second marriage

1974, In England

1981, 30<sup>th</sup> birthday

1985, In Iran

1990, In Australia

1995, Third marriage

2001, 50th birthday

2005, University of Wollongong graduation

2011, At my 60<sup>th</sup> birthday I looked 40 and I felt 20.
But when I was 20, I looked 40 and I felt 60

Victoria with her twin soul mate (husband)